Alan Warner's
Morvern Callar

T0347888

CONTINUUM CONTEMPORARIES

Also available in this series

Pat Barker's *Regeneration*, by Karin Westman
Kazuo Ishiguro's *The Remains of the Day*, by Adam Parkes
Carol Shields's *The Stone Diaries*, by Abby Werlock
J.K. Rowling's *Harry Potter Novels*, by Philip Nel
Jane Smiley's *A Thousand Acres*, by Susan Farrell
Barbara Kingsolver's *The Poisonwood Bible*, by Linda Wagner-Martin
Irvine Welsh's *Trainspotting*, by Robert Morace
Donna Tartt's *The Secret History*, by Tracy Hargreaves
Toni Morrison's *Paradise*, by Kelly Reames
Don DeLillo's *Underworld*, by John Duvall
Annie Proulx's *The Shipping News*, by Aliki Varvogli
Graham Swift's *Last Orders*, by Pamela Cooper
Haruki Murakami's *The Wind-up Bird Chronicle*, by Matthew Strecher
Ian Rankin's *Black and Blue*, by Gill Plain
Michael Ondaatje's *The English Patient*, by John Bolland
Bret Easton Ellis's *American Psycho*, by Julian Murphet
Cormac McCarthy's *All the Pretty Horses*, by Stephen Tatum
Iain Banks's *Complicity*, by Cairns Craig
A.S. Byatt's *Possession*, by Catherine Burgass
David Guterson's *Snow Falling on Cedars*, by Jennifer Haytock
Helen Fielding's *Bridget Jones's Diary*, by Imelda Whelehan
Sebastian Faulks's *Birdsong*, by Pat Wheeler
Kate Atkinson's *Behind the Scenes at the Museum*, by Emma Parker
Hanif Kureishi's *The Buddha of Suburbia*, by Nahem Yousaf
Nick Hornby's *High Fidelity*, by Joanne Knowles
Zadie Smith's *White Teeth*, by Claire Squires
Arundhati Roy's *The God of Small Things*, by Julie Mullaney
Margaret Atwood's *Alias Grace*, by Gina Wisker
Vikram Seth's *A Suitable Boy*, by Angela Atkins

Forthcoming in this series

Jonathan Coe's *What a Carve Up!*, by Pamela Thurschwell
Louis De Bernieres's *Captain Corelli's Mandolin*, by Con Coroneos

· **ALAN WARNER'S**

Morvern Callar

A READER'S GUIDE

SOPHY DALE

CONTINUUM | NEW YORK | LONDON

2002

The Continuum International Publishing Group Inc
370 Lexington Avenue, New York, NY 10017

The Continuum International Publishing Group Ltd
The Tower Building, 11 York Road, London SE1 7NX

www.continuumbooks.com

Library of Congress Cataloging-in-Publication Data

Dale, Sophy.
  Alan Warner's Morvern Callar : a reader's guide / by Sophy Dale.
    p. cm. — (Continuum contemporaries)
  Includes bibliographical references (p.) and index.
  ISBN 0-8264-5328-7 (pbk. : alk. paper)
  1. Warner, Alan. Morvern Callar. I. Title. II. Series.
PR6073.A7227 M6733 2002
823'.914—dc21
                         2002000877

Contents

1.
The Novelist   7

2.
The Novel   21

3.
The Novel's Reception   68

4.
The Novel's Performance   73

5.
Further Reading and Discussion Questions   82

Acknowledgments

Many thanks to Robin Robertson and, especially, to Alan Warner

The Novelist

BIOGRAPHICAL DETAILS

Alan Warner was born in Oban, Scotland, in 1964. His father was from Yorkshire, his mother from the Isle of Mull. (They met in Central Europe in the aftermath of World War II.) He grew up in the hotel that his parents ran in a village a few miles outside Oban, the model for "the Port" in his novels. He left school as soon as he could and went to work on the railways, but later did evening classes and then attended university in London, before coming back to Scotland to do a postgraduate degree at Glasgow University (his thesis was on Joseph Conrad). After that, he had a variety of jobs, including working in supermarkets, before the success of his first novel enabled him to give up the "day job." He now lives with his wife in Ireland and has published four novels, of which *Morvern Callar* (1995) is the first.

With the Lynne Ramsay film adaptation of *Morvern Callar* and an adaptation of *The Sopranos* on the horizon, and the critical and commercial successes of his novels, Warner feels privileged to be in a position where he's not pressured to keep churning out books before he's ready, and is able just to write and not to have to have a day job—"When I was first published I lived with the nightmare that I'd have to go back to work in a month's time, and in a way that hasn't left me. I'm starting to feel that it'll be years not months, but I still don't take the luxury of having all this time for granted."[1]

INFLUENCES

I first interviewed Alan Warner two years ago, for a piece which appeared in the *Edinburgh Review*, in which he discussed his influences at length. Much of this section of the book is based on our conversations at that time, focusing particularly on the influence of Scottish writers (which is also discussed in the section on "Language" later in the book). Warner's range of literary reference is extremely broad, taking in North American writers such as Melville, Dos Passos, Mark Richard, Annie Proulx, Michael Ondaatje, and a whole host of European writers such as Camus, Sartre, Gide, Beckett, Joyce, Gogol, and Cervantes, along with Scottish writers. Interestingly, the only English writer I've ever heard him mention approvingly is Emily Brontë (quoted in the epigraph to *The Sopranos*), a writer greatly concerned with landscape, adolescent passions, extreme emotions, heightened realism, dialect, and narrators who withhold or deny their emotions—all features to be found in Warner's own writing, as this book will go on to discuss.

Among Scottish influences, there are a number who stand out: Hugh MacDiarmid, Lewis Grassic Gibbon, James Kelman, Tom Leonard, James Kennaway, and Iain Crichton Smith. Warner says that the rural settings of Grassic Gibbon's novels were particularly important as a contrast to the urban-centric novels of the 1980s:

But it was really Duncan McLean's first collection of stories *Bucket of Tongues*, that was the final piece in the jigsaw. When I read those rural stories in there in 1993: "Bed of Thistles" and that wonderful long dark one "Hours of Darkness" which was like something out of Turgenev, I was just overwhelmed. Cause of course *Morvern Callar* was a completed manuscript in my Clark's shoebox by this time and I just read Duncan's book with astonishment, thinking that here was fantastic Scottish writing but lots of it was based away from the urban places, it was set in the geographical peripheries and it was published! I just realised maybe *Morvern* was acceptable then; I really thought it was just beyond the pale that novel, it would never be published but then of course all this other great writing was appearing, Irvine's first stuff, urban though it was, suddenly a culture I recognised, a culture of skateboarders and drug use and football casuals and three day drinking, like in Duncan's wonderful, existentialist story, "Lucky to be Alive," and of course contemporary rural Scotland; it was all just there and it was a wonderful time this, in 1993, and Duncan was my own age and I'd never met a writer my own age before — so Duncan loved *Morvern* and it was him who convinced me to send off the manuscript. So in a way Duncan is the hugest influence who in turn was very influenced by James Kelman.

Going back to his schooldays, the literary influences Warner remembers most clearly from English lessons were:

for drama, *Who's Afraid Of Virginia Woolf?* — I saw the Burton/Taylor film version and was electrified by it. Poetry was "Anthem for Doomed Youth" and Edwin Morgan. The novel was *Consider the Lilies*, which was strange, because Iain Crichton Smith taught at the school. God, what a wonderful man he was! We did *Heart of Darkness* and also *The House with the Green Shutters*, which of course I consider one of the great Scottish masterpieces. It had a big effect on me . . . that scene where young Gourlay passes the carpenters . . . Edwin Morgan's *Selected Poems* delighted me — and I bought two poetry records: Sorley Maclean and Edwin Morgan and Alex Scott reading their poems.

Iain Crichton Smith told the young Warner about a Sorley Maclean reading at the Columba hall in Oban:

I was intimidated about going, I thought it would be in Gaelic, but it was very friendly and it changed my life. Sorley read in English and Gaelic and Iain Crichton Smith read from some of the Murdo stories. This would be about 1981 I would think, and it had a huge effect on me—I started investigating Scottish literature from then on, discovering more. I was totally starstruck by it all—not that Sorley and Iain were particularly glamorous!—but when you heard them read and Sorley's voice and you read about Sorley and his life, you realised what a moral giant he was. It snowballed pretty rapidly as I tried to get hold of world literature. It was traumatic in that it drove me away from Oban, the more I read, the more I believed I had to leave to study literature, to become something and the repercussions of that are still going on for me. Books do change things, not necessarily always for the good, and they do change lives. I read Gide's *The Immoralist* and moved from there to Camus, Sartre and the whole existentialist tradition and all these other countries started to open up. Internationalism is so important—you can't arrive at your own style just through the local any more, not since modernism. You might start with the local, and it's very important but you can't arrive at everything you need without reading beyond the local.

Warner's immense respect for his literary antecedents does not, however, go alongside a veneration of the academic study of literature:

It's a regret of mine now that I bothered going to university. I mean, literally I benefitted so much because I could get my hands on books and records that I couldn't have got otherwise, but I still regret that I felt I needed to go. I was reading the books that were on the reading lists but I was reading three or four times as many books around that—and of course it bought me leisure time away from the job so I could read more—so that side of it, the sheer practicalities of being able to read more, was very important. But as for the actual engagement with writing essays and the pearls of wisdom that came scuttering off the table from my lecturers, I'm not so sure about that at all—I mean, the gurus that I had in life were a couple of guys and a girl back home in Oban—they remain my gurus now, much smarter folk than me, they should be winning awards, not me. Guys like Kenny Lindsay the actor and Neil Morrison, guys from the council estate, but I didn't grew up on a council estate. These guys were real working class intellectuals, you know Kenny was reading Sean O'Casey's autobiographies when he was seventeen years old, and our mate Bob who's a lawyer now, and me were into Neitzsche when I was fifteen, so we were precocious in that way, round in each others' bedrooms, watery Nescafé and digestives, listening to Miles Davis and The Gang of Four and The Fall and discussing Borges, I mean I learned more from those guys in a couple years than I ever did at Uni so I don't think an English degree is an advantage at all in becoming a creative writer. I'm deeply suspicious of creative writing courses as well, despite the fact that a lot of fine writers, especially American ones, have come out of them. In Britain more seems to have come out of the more informal groups, like Philip Hobsbaum's group in Glasgow.

As readers of *These Demented Lands* discover, Morvern uses the windfall money left to her by her boyfriend to buy herself time for travel and reading, eschewing university in a manner of which you can only imagine her creator approves wholeheartedly.

During the course of the interview, we discussed the manipulation of the narrative voice by a number of writers whom Warner sees as particularly influential. In particular, we discussed Gogol, a huge influence on the teenaged Warner, who at fifteen had just discovered the spellbinding power of the written word. The unstable narrative world described by Gogol is one which has echoes of the way in which the material world fascinates Morvern, but remains forever outside her grasp, impossible to pin down, since she looks at the surfaces of things, not always at the objects themselves. To take only one small example from many possibilities, she describes how, numbed with grief, she "looked at the changing lights coming from the telly and showing across the room," (47) rather than watching the television itself. Warner was astonished by the narrative liberties taken by Gogol:

Like in *Dead Souls*, Gogol just goes, Och, there's no point in me describing this weary travellers' inn in a godforsaken nowhere, it's like all the other taverns in this dump of Russia, you know them all so well reader; then he goes on to actually describe it, so you get this world weariness in the actual narrative voice, the sort of idea that nothing is new under the sun. Then he'll go, there's no real need to describe these weary servants cause you know what they're like, you know them so well, and off he goes on these big digressions and describes them. Then he'll follow a character up the road, describing what they're like then he'll just write: they have no further relevance to the story and he just dumps them! He does that on the first PAGE of *Dead Souls!* It's astonishingly brave and, more to the point, incredibly funny—these digressions are so contrary to the idea of traditional narration but they add this wonderful resonance to the novel. I mean, I think Gogol just wanted to go out for a drink, but he's literally mocking the narrator's role, he's questioning it all, "All these people are clearly mad, but so am I" is the looming subtext. And of course he was! He's such an important writer formally, compared to say Dostoyevsky. And some of Gogol's descriptions: he wasn't a tall man, neither was he short, he wasn't too heavy but I wouldn't say he was a thin man! all these mad, unnerving statements are just made, everything is so unstable. Kafka must have studied that, cause you can see the indeterminacy right there too.

Of course, in Morvern's case, far from being the blasé "party chick" described by some of the book's critics, she is anything but world-weary—instead she is hungry for experience. Rather than feeling, like Gogol's narrative voice, that there is nothing new under the sun, for Morvern *everything* is new, she sees things fresh. Partly this is due to the shock and alienation of bereavement, partly after that to the newness of having a disposable income, but the effect is of a narrative voice at once denying emotion by refusing to discuss it, but suffused with wonder at the feeling of water on the skin or the play of light on the hills. The coolness of Morvern's tone is in such stark contrast to the melodramatic events of the plot (suicide, dismembering etc.) as to create an enormous narrative tension — and then there's the number of conflicting authors buried in this text — Morvern, her dead boyfriend, and Warner himself. Destabilizing the narrative voice, then, was a lesson learned early in Warner's reading patterns:

Dead Souls was one of the first weighty Penguin Classics I read so I didn't question all that, but I really think it put a big seed in me, that when a novel is narrated it's almost certainly about the narrator and that follows right through, it's in *Wuthering Heights*, so many dodgy viewpoints, and *Benito Cerino* by Melville, what a masterpiece, so mysterious, to the Beckett trilogy. Gogol or Benito Perez Galdos, the 19th century Spaniard are so much more sophisticated than what Dickens or Thackeray were doing, so you see, the Herr Professors won't attack those works, but the narrative liberation, the tradition of what I'm doing right now, those formal achievements have a clear historical existence, so all your onanistic protectors of the canon will go "Oh, we must protect these hallowed masterpieces", yet reading those writers gave me all the ideas of what I'm doing. All the reasons for my prose can be traced through these earlier writers. The seeds of the form's implosion are always contained in earlier forms and nationalistic canons just set up non-existent barriers to development.

Juan Carlos Onetti is a huge and very complex influence, he was doing stuff before Beckett, in *The Pit* in 1939 and you could bring in Roberto Arlt too, in the twenties, where the narrator just gets fed up with the story he's telling and changes over to another one, saying someone may have been called this or this, what does it matter.

One writer's influence on another can of course operate at a number of levels, not necessarily all literary. As Warner says:

For instance as far as Scottish writers go, James Kennaway has been an enormous influence on me but there's an interesting distinction here. Kennaway: his tragic life and lifestyle, the interplay between Kennaway's life and art had a big influence on my concept of what a writer, and indeed a Scottish writer should be like, dynamic I guess, but I suppose I was drawn to it cause of course it was hopelessly glamorous in my mind then; so there was a non-intellectual romantic attachment, like to Hemingway and what he means to a male writer, that macho mythology—but Kennaway, his novels got bought by the film world and he got caught up in Hollywood. In *Tunes of Glory* and especially *Household Ghosts*, he was writing about rural Scotland which I identified with, as in Grassic Gibbon, while in *The Bells of Shoreditch* and *Some Gorgeous Accident* he was writing about Scots in London which is where I was at the time. But then his fictional world was a pretty middle class one and he'd gone to Glenalmond private school and Oxford and all that which I felt very intimidated by, at that time.
     You know I had a very comfortable upbringing, never wanted for anything and my parents were well off, but I never felt middle class, to me middle class was sort of, not swearing in the house, saying grace or speaking French and knowing what wines to drink with what and going to private school instead of a comprehensive, or having piano lessons or lots of books and classical music in the house. Like, we had no books in the house to talk of, an AA map and some boring encyclopedias and a great Hank Williams record that belonged to my folks. Kennaway was all that Perthshire gentry society where folk are related to aristocrats and all that. You know my old man was an ex-sergeant major, a Yorkshireman from Sheffield steel town, "sunset floosh" was sort of his idea of a good painting y'know? So that upper class stuff in Kennaway was foreign to me and I think this has worked against him as far as his critical standing in Scotland goes. He was a bit like Trocchi weirdly, perhaps too international and outward looking, perhaps even too flamboyant to become part of the Scottish canon; there again since Compton Mackenzie and Gavin Maxwell are so comfortably part of it perhaps that's odd? But maybe since Kennaway's death in

1968, the urban, working class was starting to re-emerge in Scottish writing, and quite rightly, through Tom Leonard and say an amazing story, like Jeff Torrington's "The Last Shift" so Kennaway got kinda submerged in that. Anyway I think Kennaway's obscurity is a great loss for Scotland. Then similarly flamboyant you had Hugh MacDiarmid who I had to work my way through just to get past him!

When it comes to James Kelman's work, Warner says, "his influence can't be underestimated — I don't think I could have had the courage to write if I hadn't just glanced over a single page of Kelman. You just had to look at a page and see there's a whole spectrum of things you could draw from it. I shelve his books beside Beckett." In some ways, however, Warner sees himself as reacting against Kelman — perhaps most notably by turning away from Kelman's admirable refusal just to "tell stories." Indeed, he sees this as:

a reaction against the lack of narrative drive in most twentieth-century Scottish novels. I read Robin Jenkins or Iain Crichton Smith a lot, and they are very important to me, but sometimes I found them furiously slow, not much happening. *Consider the Lilies* is a very important book to me, but it's urbanely paced. A lot of my own writing is a reaction against the Beckett thing and James Kelman's beautiful ability to tell a story in which nothing happens — that fantastic one in *Greyhound for Breakfast*, "Even in communal pitches," where the guy just shifts position at a party where he can't get settled but it comes across as this huge, reverberating life changing, existential statement — it's so good.

I don't think that I'm a good enough writer to write a story like that. It's not that I'd criticise Beckett or Kelman, I love their work so much, but of course, when you have, say Beckett's final work, *Stirrings Still*, where just a hand moves in the entire, wonderful narrative, or the narrative voice tries to recall a word . . . and fails, there is nowhere left to go, especially for a lesser writer like me. Kelman's so involved in language and breathing, I heard him read "The one with the dog" one time in San Francisco, and I was just sat there listening to all the richness, all the infinite implications of the Glasgow voice, coming forth: like the character is the voice of a jackey, a wino, just sounding off and it was so overwhelmingly great, seriously, it was like Homer or something and that story "Old Francis" . . . it's just this old guy on a park bench and these guys come along, real sinister men, but when I read that story . . . it's just so infinitely sinister, like these guys are all the evil in the world and Old Francis is the only good, trying to hold out. In fact it was that story that gave me the courage to compress "Offof" into a perfectly valid word. I mean we use that word everyday but it's not in the dictionary and Kelman is trying to disgorge up as much of the vocabulary as he can. Every sentence has his signature on it and that's very hard to do.

Big florid things that are I would imagine, anathema to James Kelman's art, happen all the time in *Morvern Callar*—horses swimming to girls on beaches and so on. To James Kelman I believe that's just beyond the pale, his work is so specifically committed, in the best sense. But there again you have these surreally beautiful pieces of his, like "Roofsliding" and that one where the guy walks out of the sea, so who knows.

The influence of writers such as Kelman or Duncan McLean was interrupted by the period of three years when Warner was out of Scotland while he was at university in London:

I went down to college in London in 1984 and returned in Summer 1987 to attend Glasgow Uni on a postgraduate course, I was writing a thesis on Conrad. Robert Crawford [the poet—now Professor of Scottish Literature at the University of St. Andrews] was a young lecturer there and he was great, very interesting, talking about Dracula in *The Waste Land*, making it interesting. Philip Hobsbaum [an academic with an awesome reputation for setting up creative writing groups—Seamus Heaney was in his Belfast group, and Alasdair Gray, Tom Leonard, James Kelman, and Liz Lochhead met at his Glasgow group] was there who knew Heaney of course so I was sort of in awe of him but he sussed I was a closet writer and was kind to me. That was quite a crucial time—and when I was down in London I was really very much out of touch with what was going on in Scotland. For instance, Duncan McLean was very much involved in the Merry Macs during that period, but by the time I came back to Scotland they'd broken up and I didn't have a clue that they'd existed—that theatre group and that agit-prop comedy style. I thought Duncan had always been a janitor when I met him—I didn't know he'd done that in the past. For reading Kelman that was a pretty crucial time, *Greyhound for Breakfast* had come out but it was before *A Disaffection*—I was in London when *Busconductor Hines* and *A Chancer* were coming out—and I missed those books. I didn't read them until I came back up. All I had was *Not Not While the Giro* which I found quite difficult in places, but there were two crucial stories in there, "Nice to be nice" (the one that's written phonetically, like "Honest," by Tom Leonard) and "The Bevel." "The Bevel" was very important cause, like that strange one "The Red Cockatoos," it's set in the countryside which again is an issue cause much as Kelman's voice and Leonard's voice were incredibly important they also were so intensely urban and I didn't come from that background. And they were alienating in the sense that Tom Leonard's poems are often about not having any subject for the poem, it's wonderfully IN the language itself—and increasingly for Kelman, from *A Chancer* onwards, it was less and less narrative driven. There was a political point to that, he thinks narrative is bourgeois because it implies that you have material security—there's so much drama in having no material security that it's an act of bad faith on his part to invent elaborate plots—and there's definitely a reaction to that in *Morvern Callar*.

Alongside Kelman and Leonard, another important influence whom Warner sees as having a huge effect on the way he writes is that self-made Colossus of twentieth-century Scottish literature, MacDiarmid. Countless Scottish writers have found MacDiarmid's influence to be almost paralyzing, but for Warner it was liberating in that it offered the freedom of making up your own language:

Above Kelman and Leonard was this idea of synthetic language from MacDiarmid, that you could take all different bits of language and use them. Like the word "bonzo" in *Morvern Callar*. It was a word my mother used for the dustbin in the house—I thought it was an obscure Scots word from her rural upbringing. My Grandad was a landworker, ditch digger, working on big landed estates draining land and planting trees then later he was a tenant farmer, so my Mother, who came from a family of thirteen kids, had this incredibly beautiful vocabulary of Scots terms and phrases; so I thought bonzo was this old, respected word for an ashbucket, which in itself is an old term for a dustbin, but apparently I named the dustbin bonzo when I was a kid because I couldn't pronounce bin, so I called it bonzo!! It was like a family word. It's a great one for testing out the foreign translators that! And *Morvern's* been put into most of the European languages so we always have a laugh with the translators about that one!! In *Morvern Callar* I was using all kinds of different words from different places and pushing words together. Also I was using them to distance things and to make them non-specific — the colours are always green*ish* or gold*ish*, no one's quite sure and this non-specificity creates a power.

OTHER WORKS

So far, Warner has published three further novels, the first of which, *These Demented Lands*, is a sequel to *Morvern Callar*. He always planned that there should be a trilogy of Morvern books, but is now less sure about publishing the third (which he had intended would be the book that Morvern's boyfriend has written, and which she publishes under her own name). The critics are somewhat divided on the issue of *These Demented Lands*, which some consider to be Warner's masterpiece, while others think it is overly ambitious and too disjointed and hallucinogenic in style. It picks up Morvern's story at the point at which *Morvern Callar* leaves off, with the pregnant and penniless Morvern setting off for the Island (Mull) where it has been suggested that she might be able to get a job in a remote hotel. However, the boat taking her over from the mainland sinks (on the first page of the book) and it is left unclear whether Morvern has died and the rest of the novel is taking place in the underworld, or whether she has in fact survived, and the Island is simply deeply eccentric.

Like *Morvern*, it is told in the first person, but in this case there are two narrators and multiple found texts, from posters and rock family trees to letters—the staple narrative device used since the birth of the novel. In the course of the book, Morvern travels through the Alice in Wonderland-esque world of the Island, in which characters speak in riddles and perform rituals as potentially dangerous as the court games of the Queens and Duchesses in *Alice*, while inversions are everywhere (there's a memorable drag party). Among the first people Morvern meets on the island are the almost identical brothers, First Spoken and Most Baldy, reminiscent of Tweedledum and Tweedledee. She describes the island as "crazy . . . like a dream," and meets a character (Aircrash Investigator) who has been set an impossible task. The terrain across which she travels also has much in common with Bunyan's moral landscape in *Pilgrim's Progress* (which Warner remembers being read to him in an abridged version at primary school), while the scenes of her starving on the heath recall Lear and the Fool in *King Lear* or Jane's flight from Rochester in *Jane Eyre*. Most strongly, however, as the epigraph's quote from *Kidnapped* highlights, it recalls David Balfour's flight across the strange moral landscape of Mull, meeting blind catechists and other equally unhelpful guides as he goes.

The timeless and otherworldly qualities to *Demented Lands* form a contrast to Warner's third novel, *The Sopranos*, set partly in the Port and partly in the Capital (Edinburgh), and grounded throughout in the quotidian world of McDonald's, HMV, and the last dance at the disco. In the chronology of Warner's fictional world, *The Sopranos* comes before *Morvern Callar*—one character refers to Morvern toward the end of *The Sopranos* and it is clear that at this stage she is still living with the boyfriend in their flat, before his suicide. The reviews were almost unanimous in their praise for

Warner's ear for teenage girls' dialogue—as Polly Rance put it in *The Richmond Review*:

This is a novel for anyone who has ever been a teenage girl. Its accuracy is staggering. Alan Warner has somehow managed to tap into the insanity and hysteria of adolescent femininity and depicts it with vigour and tenderness. (*www.richmondreview.co.uk/books/soprano.html*)

Like *Morvern Callar*, *The Sopranos* is being adapted for film, in this case by Scottish director Michael Caton Jones (whose other films include *Rob Roy* and *This Boy's Life*). Finally, there's Warner's most recent novel, *The Man Who Walks*, a picaresque tale of a homeless young drifter's pursuit of his uncle, the eponymous Man Who Walks, around a slightly surreal Scotland, patrolled by Hollywood producers, ex-British Rail trolley girls, crazed Buddhist snowboarders, and a sybaritic aristocracy.

2

The Novel

LANGUAGE

Language, of course, always carries a political freight, an issue which Warner's forerunners in Scotland have not shied away from. There is no such thing as "neutral" language — a writer either chooses to write in the language of power — Standard English in Britain — or not, but either way, the choice is inescapably a politicized one. Hugh MacDiarmid, for instance, saw his creation of "synthetic Scots" as a national duty, while James Kelman and the poet Tom Leonard (an avowed admirer of *Morvern Callar*) have written passionately of their political commitment to the depiction of speech on the page. In his essay, "On Reclaiming the Local," Leonard writes:

The most obvious area where the writer is usually patronising is in the depiction of speech, where for instance a writer-narrator presents standard English, and a quoted character-persona presents something else. Those apostrophes that indicate the 'and of the writer 'elping out the reader, indicating by sign the prescriptive norm from which a "character" is "deviating". The character can't talk proper words, so the writer-narrator indicates where there's bits missed out, so you can better understand. The apostrophes indicate a supposed deficiency which the reader, over the head of the persona as it were, must supply. The personae are trapped within the closed value-system that denigrates their use of language, while the writer-narrator communicates with the reader over their heads. (Leonard, 1995, p. 40)

This is precisely what Warner's narrative voice in *Morvern Callar* does *not* do. While in fact Morvern's voice, as represented on the page, looks less "different" from the perceived norm than, for instance, Mark Renton's narrative voice in Irvine Welsh's *Trainspotting* or Leonard's narrative voice in poems such as his "Unrelated Incidents" sequence, this is the result of Warner adhering more closely than Welsh or Leonard to standard orthography—he rarely alters the standard spelling of a word in order to indicate a precise pronunciation, instead using standard orthography to represent those occasions when Morvern uses a slightly different word from the norm (as for instance, "sideyways" rather than "sideways" or "blackishness" rather than "blackness" or compound words such as "far-away-like" or "out-the-game"). Occasionally, spelling does make a gesture toward a non-Received Pronunciation voice, as in "soaken" for "soaking" or "cmon" for "come on," but much more often it is syntax and vocabulary which combine to suggest a particular dialect and therefore imply an attendant accent. When Warner does alter the spelling of a word to indicate its pronunciation, this tends to be done sparingly but consistently, so that, for instance, "no" is usually represented as "nut" and "not" as "no." One of his most characteristic coinages is "offof", as in "Miles Davis doing He Loved Him Madly offof Get Up With It was going in the ears" (p. 5)—a word, or more precisely, two compressed words, frequently heard but rarely represented in print. There is an informality to the narrative voice, which finds expression in a number of ways, such as the fact that Morvern frequently omits the definite article: "Puddles were frozen and wee-ones off from school had burst all ice" (p. 5). This sentence adheres to standard spelling and contains no very unusual coinages, although "wee-ones" for "children" is both informal and suggests Scottish rather than English vocabulary—but it is the lack of "the's" which suggests the natural rhythms of speech rather than the prescriptive use of grammatical rules.

The whole novel is narrated in Morvern's voice, without the use of apostrophes or other punctuation markers nodding, as Leonard would have it, over the character-persona's head to the reader. As a result, the issue of the writer/narrator patronizing the dialect-speaking character does not occur, since Morvern's narrative voice speaks the same language as most of her characters. It is worth noting that when, in *The Sopranos*, Warner writes in the third person, his narrator's voice has a similar register to Morvern's—like all his characters, his "objective" narrator speaks in the voice of the Port. Like Grassic Gibbon and Kelman before him, Warner does not use quotation marks in *Morvern Callar* to indicate his characters' speech, thus blurring the line between "spoken" and "written" even further. However, there is a slightly higher incidence of obviously verbal shorthand in the reported speech, with the inclusion of non-standard words such as "suffish" for "sufficient" or "donks" for "donkeys' years," strengthening the impression of the faithful representation of the spoken word. Nevertheless, even in the novel's narrative voice, as distinct from reported speech, Morvern/Warner gives the impression of simply recording verbatim a story exactly as it would be told verbally—the language is mimicking the effect of the transcript of a monologue, rather than the different register of a written text. This is not to say that the language is any way lacking in complexity—indeed, it is both complex and poetic—simply that it is structured much less formally than is conventional in a written text.

If Leonard's poetry and essays helped to blaze the trail for Warner's writing, James Kelman's mastery of the third-person demotic narrative voice has also been an enormous inspiration for Warner, and the mystification with which critics and journalists greeted his work has also been instructive. Warner speaks of his surprise when watching a post-Booker prize television interview between Kelman and Mark Lawson, in which Lawson referred to the "interior monologue" in *How Late It Was, How Late* and even when corrected by Kelman, seemed unable to grasp that a narrative written in a Glaswegian voice could possibly be written in the third person. What worried Warner was "the implications of this misunderstanding . . . Lawson couldn't read that book—he was as helpless as a child before it . . . he simply couldn't distinguish the narrative voice." Amid all the knee-jerk reactions against Kelman's use of the word "fuck" in the novel, even the liberal voice of *Guardian*-reading metropolitan England, while able to overcome the multiple inclusions of "fuck," was thrown off course much more significantly, not so much by the words themselves as by the rhythms and accent in which they were written. As the Scottish novelist Alison Kennedy said in a recent interview in *Edinburgh Review*:

A lot of the reviews that complained about the language were actually complaining about the type of people who were being portrayed because they weren't the type of people who would be allowed in a "nice" novel. We've always had a linguistic debate but what they were having was "you're elevating people to the novel who aren't middle class, and that's just not allowed." So it's always "grim" or "gritty" or whatever and it's like, "No, it's just people you wouldn't have dinner with." It's a very very small world. In literary London, in the reviewing culture, it's very class-based still . . . the problem with Kelman was never that he said "Fuck," it was that he wrote about the wrong kind of people. (*Edinburgh Review*, 1999, 104)

In his introduction to the Picador anthology of contemporary Scottish writing, Peter Kravitz gives some sense of Kelman's influence on those writers most usually spoken of within the same breath as Warner:

McLean says, "When *The Busconductor Hines* came out in 1984 it just blew my mind. It was the voice. For the first time I was reading a book about the world I lived in. I didn't know literature could do that."

Welsh also credits Kelman with "setting the whole thing out so that people like myself can have more fun." A. L. Kennedy has said that people like John Byrne, Tom Leonard and James Kelman "made my generation of writers possible . . . gave us permission to speak . . . made us more ourselves—gave us the reality, life and dignity that art can at a time when anything other than standard English and standard address was frowned upon." (Kravitz, 1997, p. xxiii)

Warner, in common with Welsh, Kennedy, and the rest of their generation of writers, was able to take the example of Kelman, Leonard, and others to write with confidence outside of standard English, without bowing down to the Academy's notions of "correctness," in literary writing.

Few things are more calculated to raise Warner's hackles than the subject of "correctness." By way of example, he quotes the Irish novelist John Banville's review of *The Penguin Book of Twentieth Century Essays* in *The Irish Times*. Banville writes:

Lucky for Hegel that he is not alive today, to see what has become even of prose. The casting off of the chains of style, grammar, syntax, spelling that has been happening over, say, the past twenty years, can seem like a break for freedom and an access of new energies, but bad writing is bad writing, no matter how red the heart the writer wears on his sleeve. As Claudio Magris points out in his new book MICROCOSMS, people are always all too ready to march with burning brands behind the latest mountebank of the word. "Correct usage," he writes, "is a premise for moral clarity and honesty," warning that "a single misplaced comma can result in disasters." His warning should be engraved on the walls of every classroom . . . in what used to be called the civilised world.

Warner sees such a position as:

a total attack on my own and so many other writing cultures. It hurts me to have to reply harshly also, but I think anybody has a right to reply when people start claiming to be moral authorities as well as artists. I actually do believe great artists: Melville, Kafka, Camus, Joyce, Orson Welles, the Bröntes, do express great moralities through their work, but this is a gift they must let time bestow upon them, rather than claiming a right to moral authority through the middle class newspapers. So, let's just notice the intellectual subjectivity and political assumptions of what's being said by Banville here. Firstly, without qualifying what is "bad writing" it is introduced in connection with "casting off chains of . . . grammar, syntax and spelling . . ." then Banville quotes a professor of German from Trieste University. Unquestioningly we are told "correct usage" (which of course is not defined), is enshrined as an abstract representation of "moral clarity and honesty" and lo & behold, with Biblical certainty, a misplaced comma, along with writing that ignores "correct usage of grammar, syntax and spelling," is seriously accused of being dishonest and indeed, morally suspect!!! That's quite an accusation. Well, if you're a computer programmer in HTML language a misplaced comma CAN be bloody disastrous! But when it comes to literary linguistic laws of the land being imposed from up on the walls of the classrooms we're back to an oppression and elitism one had hoped had been long abandoned.

Warner continues to argue that:

By Banville's and Magris' position, the language Fionnula, Orla and Chell speak in *The Sopranos* or the narrative language used by Morvern and the Port people in *Morvern Callar* or *These Demented Lands*, is bad writing. It is not "correct usage" and is therefore contrary to moral clarity and honesty. Obviously so must be the language spoken by the characters in the work of James Kelman, or say the language spoken by Annie Proulx's characters in *Close Range* or even, say the language spoken by the characters in Faulkner's *As I Lay Dying* and if you follow the history of using the spoken language of the people, AS THE BASIS FOR WRITING, you would have to condemn Chaucer and Dante also. Of course there is always an enshrined language that represents the values of an elite status quo, which is always in opposition to the dialects, and spoken languages of the masses or/ and of linguistic minorities. Banville and Magris invent some irreconcilable gulf between Spoken Language and Written Language. I feel I wasted my time going to University and it's because I was once naïve enough to believe positions like Banville's and Magris' that I feel that way. They want to set up a whole arcane and hermetic "academy" of what constitutes "correct usage" of language and what does not. Morally improving literature can only be created by members of this academy, great literature can only be created by using definite language in a specific way, approved by certain people and all other language is thrown to the lions. And of course, this academy decides who is allowed in and who conforms to its rules.

This myth of authoritarian "correct usage" is exactly what the excerpts and highlighting of a graffito or a scribble or the use of an obscure word, or even a non-existent word is there to undercut in Warner's work. In his experience, people simply do not speak in finely constructed elegant sentences:

I believe there is infinite poetry in daily language, the same way there is in Nature; I mean that's where so-called refined language came from, it all came from the everyday, the street, and was dressed up with required etiquette. I don't feel I'm butchering any language, I feel I'm going back to its honest origins. Inevitably, in writing fiction out of specific culture, you have the spoken dialogue of the characters first, but I've noticed how certain novels, an art form supposedly filled with characters, can have almost no spoken dialogue in them. It always makes my suspicious ears waggle when you get to about page three and there's been all this exposition, but nobody has spoken yet, I mean you even get it in writers I like, but it's an odd thing how spoken dialogue is pushed down into second place. You find it a lot in intellectually playful post-modern novels. In short you get it more in the middle class novel than anywhere else because of course, the narrative voice is, unconsciously, more important than the characters. That's bad writing. If the writer feels it is appropriate, any language in any context can become part of literature.

The apparent contradiction between writing novels which are obsessed with their status as texts (including postcards, maps, road signs, etc.), but are also testaments to a belief in the power of spoken language and oral culture, is not one which has escaped Warner:

It's funny how language is so important in Scottish literature and it's so important to me — we're all so obsessed with regional variations or dialect or perhaps even suspect concepts of authenticity and purity of certain local languages whatever — it's such a major issue, and everyone's so touchy about it, like gender, and yet that goes alongside being so obsessed with the artefacts being texts. Essentially I think I'm more prickly and suspect about language. I hope I'm not over-precious about it cause I do believe its an infinitely renewable resource. I do get depressed that dialect is being lost, say from the predominantly agrarian cultures of Scotland and Ireland by increasing urban domination, MTV soundbites affecting kids' speech patterns and all that but Christ, it's not progress, but it is the forward movement of reality. You can't stop language changing, which is the problem with that Lallans preciousness and "correct" spelling lobbies.

And though I'm not a Gael, I have the liberal's sense of protectiveness about that incredible language but I pray for a huge, great, modern Gaelic novel. If a young Scottish Gael could do something now in prose like Sorley Maclean did in poetry. Imagine!! I really think the young Turks of the Gaeltacht owe it to that culture to run to the typewriters. Self-important as it seems, I've been thinking, out of my own pocket, of financing a Gaelic translation of *Morvern Callar*, maybe even making textual changes to it to make Morvern a Gael! Cause it's clear she's not a Gaelic speaker but when I was writing it I had bizarre ideas of bringing that in somehow. I was seriously thinking of publishing the work through a small press or something but I guess that's just a pipedream.

Both concerns—representing spoken language and playing games with textuality—can be seen within the work of nineteenth-century Scottish writers, with Scott pioneering the representation of dialect in the novel (not of course in the narrative voice, but present in his characters' dialogue), and basing much of his writing on the oral culture of ballads and folk tales; and Stevenson and Carlyle and Hogg, posing as editors of texts consisting of multi-authored letters, memoirs, diaries, and legal documents. Neither of these concerns are by any means exclusive to Scottish writers, but they do seem to have been more prominent in Scottish writing than, for instance, in English writing over the same period. Warner's contemporaries in Scotland share his preoccupation with multiple voices and textuality—issues which are explored for instance in Alasdair Gray's *Poor Things* or Janice Galloway's *The Trick Is to Keep Breathing*.

One of Warner's prime concerns has been to represent the power of oral culture, and his novels are filled with stories and anecdotes that his characters tell one another, from Couris Jean telling Morvern of the horses on the beach that struck her dumb for four years to the tales told by Red Hanna or the Panatine in the bar. His characters' nicknames contain stories in themselves. To quote from a section early on in the novel, when Morvern is looking around to see who's already arrived in The Mantrap, she reels off a long list of nicknames, of which the following is only an extract, revealing a playfully witty community wordplay:

. . . Cheese, whos called Suds since he started washing, Yellow Pages, The Dai Lama, Weed, Jimmy Gobhainn, that Four by Fours daughter, Marine

Girl, The Seacow, a couple of the Dose brothers, that hippy girl Snowballs at the Moon, The Scoular, Synchro, Offshore, Smiler and Hailey ... (p. 15)

In contrast to the Port's vibrant storytelling culture, Morvern finds a different — and impoverished — oral culture when she goes down to London. Ironically, perhaps it is two publishers, who make their living from the dissemination of *written* culture, who are described thus: "Tom and Susan ... didn't tell stories they just discussed" (p. 164). As Warner says:

The nicknames of the people in town — Tequila Sheila, the Argonaut — are the manifestations of a very strong confident culture — kind of poetic, you get that all the time; in any pub in the Highlands late on a Saturday, you'll hear a sequence of stories better than any Henry James novel. Well, maybe not in Fort William!

There are no artists, bookish people or intellectuals in the The Port in *Morvern Callar* (apart from Morvern's boyfriend, and he's deid!), but the stories of the culture are very strong — the horses coming up the beach, even the scatological tales, or the guy who gets crushed between the railway wagons — cause that was very much my position — I don't mean trapped between railway wagons but trapped in this silence imposed on me by obsessions with Correct Usage of language, and illusions as to what a writer, especially a male writer, should be; sorta shut out of literary culture, but I thought these stories I had were as good as any other culture's stories ... I think the move to the third person in *The Sopranos* is a sign of confidence in the language I'm working in that I'm not sure is there in the first two books. I'm not saying that aesthetically I have worries about them, it's just a change of daring.

In effect, what Warner sees as having happened by the time he came to write *The Sopranos* was a greater confidence that allowed him to let go of the device of the first person voice and to move instead to the third person, without recourse to the standard English and the all-seeing, all-powerful eye of the narratives of Waugh, Greene, or Henry James, whose novels he finds alienating.

It is of course easy to forget that England's monolinguistic culture is unusual to the point of being almost unique — most countries in the world (for instance, Spain, with Spanish, Basque, and Catalan; or Germany with "high" and "low" German; French or Flemish in Belgium; the multiple languages of India, most African nations, etc.) are in a situation much more similar to that of Scotland, with its three languages of English, Scots, and Gaelic (although the arguments as to when Standard Scottish English becomes Scots, and indeed as to whether Scots is a language or a collection of dialects will still be reverberating around the ivory towers of academe for centuries to come). This fact complicates any study of the language Warner employs in *Morvern Callar* — he is not only reproducing the language of a particular social class, but also that of a regional subset of a national group, so that the differences from the perceived norm of Standard English are greater than if his supermarket workers and train drivers were living in Birmingham rather than the Highlands. On top of this is the fact that, in *Morvern Callar* as in all his published novels, Warner's central characters are young, and their language reflects this — the language of the older characters in the novel such as Couris Jean, and even Red Hanna is much more formal than that of Morvern and Lanna.

Warner, in common with James Kelman, Irvine Welsh, and many other Scottish writers, has found the language in which he writes treated with varying degrees of bafflement by English critics. As discussed above, the reasons for this bafflement have to do with issues of class as much as nationality — as can be seen particularly clearly in a review by William Fiennes which appeared in the *London Review of Books* in July 1998. The review covers Warner's first three books, and declares itself astonished that the "mandarin sensibility of an Updike or a Nabokov" should be masquerading as "the voice of an Oban shelf-stacker." Fiennes writes that "Morvern's voice has been praised for its originality, but being original is not the same as being true: her prose is a trick, an artful ventriloquism." For Fiennes, it appears that the "true" voice of a supermarket worker could not possibly express a sensibility which he describes as "exquisite". He writes that:

That sensibility becomes even more refined when Morvern travels to the Mediterranean. She looks closely at beer, noting "the constellations of minute bubbles slipping back down the inside of the cold glass that was wet with condensation." She tells us: "When I stubbed out the butt you saw the loveliness of colours: my nails, the glittery gold Sobranie filter in the ashtray with the bright, tousled strips of orange peel among": "tousled" gives the game away—the token of a literateness which the childlike solecism of that end-of-sentence "among" cannot fully conceal. She observes "peacocks' eyes of olive oil skimming atop the vinegar, dapples of black pepper and tawny streaks of mustard popped onto the biggest leaf of lettuce."

Why precisely it strikes Fiennes as unfeasible that Morvern should look closely at a glass of beer it is difficult to imagine—he complains that her language is inconsistent with her character, but in the sentences he quotes in this passage, the only word that he can single out as overtly "literary" is "tousled." Quite apart from the fact that, as he notes himself with incredulity, Morvern refers in her own texts to having read "literary" books such as Golding's *Pincher Martin*, Fiennes' assumption that "tousled" is a purely literary word reveals an ignorance of the language of women's magazines and their features on hairstyles, which is presumably the kind of reading-matter which he would consider to be entirely suitable for Morvern.

Fiennes goes on to complain that:

The style of all three novels is characterised by the conjunction of the colloquial with the high aesthetic. Morvern used a series of vivid Scottish synonyms: not crying but *greeting*, not sexy but *rampant*, not drunk but *mortal*, not armpits but *oxters*, not vomit but *boak* . . . Despite the sparkle of such coinage and slang, Warner's prose [in *The Sopranos*] has not lost its tendency to Updikean preciousness . . . These two modes exist in uneasy tension. Warner quotes Malcolm Lowry. He incorporates into the narrative a line from a poem by Apollinaire . . . Meanwhile, the girls are talking about Kurt Cobain and Ricki Lake and Montel Williams and Keyser Soze from *The Usual Suspects* and the fact that Wonderbra model Eva Herzigova is married to Jon Bon Jovi's drummer. Warner's prose implies an extremely literate, aesthetic sensibility: the sopranos, one imagines, would quickly tell an aesthetic sensibility exactly what it should do with itself.

Although Fiennes' criticism here is directed specifically at *The Sopranos*, he makes it clear that he would extend it to the two earlier novels as well. He seems unaware of the implications of his distaste for the yoking together of "these two modes"—he claims that the inclusion of an aesthetic sensibility in the depiction of young working-class women is original but somehow not "true"— by which he appears to mean, not true to his own stereotype of working-class life. The girls in *The Sopranos* do indeed discuss Ricki Lake and Eva Herzigova, but their range, like Morvern's, extends beyond the minutiae of television trivia and they talk and think seriously about their responses to music, whether to go to university, and other concerns which Fiennes would surely see as dovetailing more readily with an aesthetic sensibility, but which he conveniently ignores for the sake of his argument. Either he thinks that working-class characters should not read poetry or listen to a wide range of music, or he thinks that the mass culture of television and supermodels should not be allowed to violate the inner sanctum of

Apollinaire and William Golding. Both positions seem equally elitist, based on defending monolithic middle-class and particularly English culture (the "colloquial" words Fiennes quotes are highlighted for their specifically Scottish nature). All in all, Fiennes appears to be made deeply uncomfortable by the fact that an author whose turn of phrase and range of reference he would be happy to admire in another context, has chosen to write about working class women's lives. As in A.L. Kennedy's take on the real problem for most English critics with James Kelman's writing, Fiennes' difficulty with Warner's novels springs from the fact that Warner is writing about "the wrong kind of people". The last word on this subject however should perhaps come from Tom Leonard's poem "Unrelated Incidents (3)" which suggests just why Fiennes might be uncomfortable with the notion that Morvern might have a "true" voice:

> *this is thi*
> *six a clock*
> *news thi*
> *man said n*
> *thi reason*
> *a talk wia*
> *BBC accent*
> *iz coz yi*
> *widny wahnt*
> *mi ti talk*
> *aboot thi*
> *trooth wia*
> *voice lik*
> *wanna yoo*
> *scruff . . .*
> *(1984, p. 88)*

SILENCE AND SENSUALITY

As a narrator, Morvern conceals her thoughts and works through indirection, such that the reader is intrigued by what she *doesn't* say, and it is this withheld emotional power, as much as the events of the plot, which compels you to read on. Warner exploits the powers of restriction by choosing a narrator whom he describes as:

inarticulate, a narrator who doesn't tell you how she feels, she maybe skirts the idea. This is a step sideways from the unreliable narrators in Gogol or Conrad [on whose work Warner wrote his post-graduate dissertation] because Morvern lies to protect herself since she's embarrassed by her feelings. Morvern's been portrayed as a party girl—well, yes, she is a party girl, but she's also quite uptight and she has problems with her emotions. By holding back all her emotions you get this big power. She holds back more and more. Christmas Day I think lasts just three brief sentences in the book—grey snow piles against the window . . .

Warner intensely dislikes filling in all the gaps in his novels:

Of course there was the whole confident ideology of the British 19th Century novel (not the Russian) which you can probably relate to class and imperialism, that everything could be rationally explained, you would go through the novel and the characters would be explicated and their behaviour would be in accordance with their character: the grand, rationalist narrative voice would lead you by the hand through all these inevitabilities to a beautifully rounded and often very moving ending; but in our time this has all been destroyed, thankfully. Gogol and Melville started it, then Conrad then the great French existential movement crushed the lie forever. I hate novels that explain everything. I wanted to leave huge silences in *Morvern Callar*—the way any sort of faith will leave us with just silence, when we gasp our last, and also to reflect Morvern's taciturn scepticism; the way the reader knows almost nothing about Morvern's boyfriend. He's perhaps middle class, or at least his old man had money, owned this hotel or perhaps there's even a hint of a criminal background or tax evasion as to where his initial money came from, the second batch of money he gives to Morvern comes from inheritance on his father's death, which also of course, seems to be some reason for his suicide. He has money but he doesn't tell Morvern.

Another interesting thing about the relationship is, what did he see in young Morvern? It's curious, it leaves a lot of questions, but I like all that. When I was working on *Morvern Callar* I fully intended to write the novel that he wrote, as part of the trilogy but now I'm not sure about that. I got a kind of power by not explaining. There are implicit comments about the relationship in the language, in the gaps—it's clear that he keeps himself to himself, but when Morvern goes to The Mantrap the others expect to see him there with her. I think he thought he'd gone everywhere and done everything, and came back to his home town to write this book, his testament or confession as a man and fell in love with this young girl—believed he's found peace of mind and she was so young at the start of their relationship that you wonder about him, you know, she was sixteen. But I think he loved her very much but perhaps as an ideal, even as a trophy to his freedom from middle class conformity. His book may be a masterpiece— the London publishers seem kind of amazed at it, but perplexed at Morvern as well. God, I would like to read it!!! I guess I'll let it be the masterwork I'll never write so it'll have its silent revenge on me after all!!! I think he thought he had it all sussed, you know, sort of intellectually, emotionally, maybe sexually too so he got too complacent and confident, let lust and old bad habits sneak up on him. It's all hinted at in his suicide note that I divide from the text and then he slept with her best friend, realised he didn't have it all sussed and something just went—one of those moral collapses that can swoop down on us all of a sudden! He realised he didn't love her enough not to sleep with Lanna, her best pal, yet is Lanna that great a pal? I think it's implicit Lanna's trying to steal him away from Morvern. Though, ironically I think it could've been easily sorted out. See I think in a way, he was uneasy about his sensuality, maybe a sort of cold, intellectual representative of Scottish Presbyterianism in a weird way, I think Morvern is a far greater sensualist than him and this is an important and often overlooked point about that novel. I think she would have easily shared Lanna with him and would have expected him to share her with another man if she wanted that. I don't think Morvern is promiscuous, I think she's a great sensualist and that's a specific difference. I think sensuality is a virtue but sensuality is more complex and has more grace than just mere sexuality or enjoyment of food or whatever. And of course, there has never been enough sensuality in Scottish writing for my tastes! Like in the poetry of Neruda or something. I love that shameless celebration of the fruits of the earth. It's always been sort of taboo in Scotland, certainly in earlier generations. It was Montaigne who wrote happiness writes white and leaves a blank page. Well much as I admire the great man's wisdom I disagree. I think in A *Happy Death* Camus wrote a very effective book about someone who dies happy and I always wanted to write a book about someone who was completely happy myself. I think *Morvern Callar* at least attempts to be a very sensual book, about someone who finds happiness for a time but is thwarted by money and society's requirement that only certain folk will be allowed happiness. Morvern is full of these awareness for Nature, for swimming, for the texture of a specific sunset, for the limitlessness of sexual athletics and why not? We all should be in this brief life. I see her boyfriend as a sort of existential figure, who was well travelled. Although he came from the middle classes, I don't think he was bourgeois. He was leading something of a double life—she didn't know how much money he had and so on, so I suppose it was a dishonest relationship in that sense, but I think it was happy nevertheless.

Morvern's sexuality has shocked some of the book's critics, but Warner sees her attitude toward sex as simply forming a part of her sensuous response to the world around her. In the letter to Red Hanna included in *These Demented Lands*, Morvern writes:

The things I've seen in the last years! Listened closely to my body and done what it told me—obviously!—and mainly otherwise read books while drinking sweet coffee all over Europe. (p. 183)

Sex, for Morvern, is simply part of the "listening closely to her body" that prompts her detailed descriptions of the feel of water as she takes a bath, or the separate tastes of olives and potatoes as she eats a meal in Spain. Frequently, sex is presented as a simple form of comfort—either for Morvern herself, as in the group sex at the party the night after she finds her boyfriend's body, where she's clearly seeking both comfort and oblivion, and indeed simply avoiding going home alone to face her boyfriend's corpse; or it is the giving of comfort, as in the hotel in Spain, when Morvern hears a man's crying from the room below her and goes downstairs to see if he's all right. Critics often describe her as "amoral" as a character, but while she certainly does not apply conventional morals either to sex or in her response to her boyfriend's suicide, she evidently has a strong personal moral code. She grieves for her boyfriend, weeps for him, prays for him, plays his music obsessively as if it could bring him back and buries him in the hills around where they had lived together. She is unfailingly kind both to Lanna and toward her work colleagues, and her anguished response on discovering that Lanna had slept with her boyfriend indicates her sense of a fierce loyalty and trust which has been betrayed. Toward older characters such as Couris Jean, she is courteous and thoughtful, and at no point in the book does she harm another living person.

Morvern instinctively shuns "fuss," which Warner sees as being intrinsic to being part of a small community, in which everyone endlessly discusses everyone else's business. She is so habitually silent, her thoughts and feelings so secret as a matter of course, that she automatically rejects the furor which would go alongside making her boyfriend's suicide public—and as soon as she walks past the phone box when she leaves the flat and doesn't ring the police or an ambulance, she is in the wrong. By doing nothing she has committed a crime, and stepped outside the law, outside society's norms. Warner points out that from an existentialist point of view she has done nothing wrong—her boyfriend is irrevocably dead and nothing she could do would change that, so there's no great moral crime in not telling the authorities and burying him herself. "Corpses are treated no better in war zones, with the tacit approval of our Governments." By stepping outside the law, however, she has become a much more interesting character. As far as the reader is concerned, she's disobeyed society's norms in a way that is shocking, and she may now go on to do anything or go anywhere—her reactions can't be predicted. Evidently, beyond her distrust of gossip is an overwhelming distrust of everyone around her, including those closest to her. As is revealed later in the novel, it transpires that Morvern is probably right not to trust either Lanna or Red Hanna, and her boyfriend has already spectacularly betrayed her faith in him. Her foster mother has died some time ago and she has no idea at all who her birth mother was, or where her biological family is from—it is hardly any wonder that she acts as if an outsider to society, given her uncertain place within it. The community within which she lives is presented as vibrant, gossipy but brutalized and impoverished emotionally as well as financially.

The first thing that Morvern writes worries her is that "all in the Port would know . . . all in the superstore would know" (p. 2)—she is driven by the desire not to be the object of gossip. She describes herself to Couris Jean as "taciturn . . . It's a word my boyfriend told me. It means you don't really say much" (p. 36). In Spain she's told that "Callar? . . . callar, ah, it means, ah, silence, to say nothing, maybe" (p. 125), although "caller" is a Scots word as well, meaning "fresh," as in the cry of street-sellers, "caller herring."

Morvern's reaction to grief is a numb silence that leads her to communicate in nods and grunts with those around her. This is clearly an extreme version of her usual "taciturn" state, since no one notices or thinks that this is odd. For the first eighteen pages of the novel, during which time she meets Creeping Jesus, Lanna,

Smugslug, Smiler, Tequila Sheila, and any number of customers whose shopping she packs, the Slab, the Panatine, Overdose, and Signal Passed at Danger, all of whom speak to her, she confines her responses to "mmm" and "uh huh." When Lanna finally cajoles her into telling the story behind her glittery knee, Morvern writes, "It was the first time I'd spoke that day if you dont count the swear-out-loud when my foot touched the blood that morning" (p. 18).

If she is habitually silent in company, and withholds her emotions even in the text which is her confession; what she writes about instead of emotion is sensation. This might be the tastes of the food she is eating, or the pulsing rhythm of the rave, or it might be the sound of a cigarette butt hissing as it is stubbed out in a pool of congealing blood. When she goes on her camping trips up into the hills to bury her boyfriend's dismembered body, she never discusses her feelings—instead she goes into great detail about the landscape and the minutiae of camping. Lanna joins her, and they go swimming, diving into a natural pool:

We hit water. Coldness punched my chest and there was a boom. Lanna pulled her hand away. I opened my eyes and saw:

Bubbles, the copperishness of the water with big bars of sun going through and through.

I surfaced beside Lanna. The wave our splash caused was cupping against the cliff and sherbety bubbles were tickling up my thighs. (p. 101)

Water, and swimming in particular, brings out Morvern's most sensuous prose, as evidenced in the many bathing scenes in the novel and, most particularly, in the night swimming section in Spain (part of which is quoted in the section "Landscape and Myth" below).

TEXTUALITY

All Warner's novels contain material other than straightforwardly typeset text, from the "hand-written" scrawl in *The Sopranos* enjoining you to "look out for limbo dancers" at the bottom of a toilet door to the inclusion of Morvern's favorite road sign in the early stages of *Morvern Callar*. In *The Sopranos*, the narrative voice muses at some length on the subject of signs taking over from language:

In McDonald's, signs were everything and language was vanishing. No words: the gender of each toilet area, the gentle admonition to deposit used trays and containers through a flap, the yellow cone, warning of slippery floors after mopping: all had no words (the sign of a stick figure, hopelessly in motion). Language was disappearing, leaving only the tokens of pounds sterling exchanged for food, a few syllables, clicked back and forth at the counter. (p. 98)

All of Warner's published novels take time to highlight the sense in which "signs were everything and language was vanishing," although as Warner says, some of his extra-narrative devices:

are there for purely formal reasons, like the leg length section at the beginning of *The Sopranos*, which seemed like the perfect trick to show all the characters, so the reader wasn't, "how many of these bastards are there?", to introduce them all in one go so that the reader wasn't confused.

The use of signs in *Morvern Callar* partly sprang from a desire on Warner's part to break the text up—as a first-time novelist, writing a book without standard chapter divisions, he was worried about potential readers being put off from reading over 200 pages of continuously flowing text. However, the inclusion of signs also foregrounds the book's textuality—acting as a defamiliarization device to disrupt the reader's relationship with the smoothly typeset text and thus to remind them of the book that they hold in their hands.

I think there is something going on in the actual typography of my writing, that I know interests you, it's a direct attack on the "status" of written literary text, how middle class literary criticism normally would value certain texts above others; how the social positioning of one text is relevant to the "authority" of the other text on the page and indeed ALL texts, you know, how certain books are valued over others, the status and class questions that must appear in any discussion of literature? Like, I've quoted, visually, graffiti in facsimile in *The Sopranos* and Red Hanna's roughly drawn map in *Morvern Callar*, road signs and hotel posters in *These Demented Lands*. And also that Rock Family Tree, that I used to introduce the character of DJ Cormorant, rather than conventionally telling you about his past, I just showed a family tree of all the rock bands he'd been in, down the years, that had this sort of sadness about it, cause all the bands were so obviously second rate! Also the rock family tree, which owes its existence to this great music critic Pete Frame, who makes these beautiful, complex trees, is in itself a sort of subversive form, cause obviously its been taken from heraldic genealogy and applied to popular music. So I visually quoted those bits of graphic "reality" onto the page and of course, they are not prose, they are sort of images but they contribute to the ongoing narrative of the story. I force what would normally be de-valued bits of text and graphics off toilet walls and wee scraps of paper INTO the prose so they take on narrative significance, become part of the art, so they cant be dismissed. When I was thinking about this recently I realised that both *Tristram Shandy* and, maybe surprisingly, Stendhal's autobiography, which featured weird typography (and I know has influenced W.G. Sebald greatly) were great influences. Now I haven't re-read these books in well over fifteen years but there are some books that just ram into your mind and you think "this is a whole concept here and some time, I'm going to use this concept." Then, lo and behold, it can be fifteen, twenty years later you just sort of nod your head and this memory of that bit of art slides out, like a drawer and just fits.

There is no language placed in a specific context that cannot become part of an aesthetic whole. Warner comments, "There should be no exclusion, surely that's the legacy of Joyce."

In this case we could take the example of the postcard Morvern and Lanna write to John and Paul, the boys they had group sex with, the night after Morvern's boyfriend has committed suicide. Morvern, who has "mused for a few secs" (p. 64) with the darkly humorous emphasis on "muse," writes her message to the two boys she has had sex with and it is shown on the page separated from the rest of the text represented as capital letters:

CHEERS FOR BUMPIN US
MORVY & LANNA
XXXXXXX

and the graffito which Lanna writes next is represented in the same way, although Warner has said that he regrets now not having had the courage to insist on a "facsimile" hand-written postcard and graffito inserted in the text, in the style of Red Hanna's map.

MORVERN CALLAR LIKES BRUTAL SEX

Morvern, clearly provoked by Lanna's words felt-tipped on the toilet cubicle door, the same way Morvern was provoked by Lanna to sleep with her and the two boys, thinks for a moment, in the classic writer's pose with the felt tip: "I bit the end a while then wrote":

LANNA PHIMISTER SAYS—SASSY SINGLE BAKERS LIKE IT BETTER FROM BEHIND. (p. 65)

Morvern's creation is more sophisticated than Lanna's, but in narrative terms it still contributes to the story because it reminds us of Lanna's single status, in contrast to Morvern. It also reminds us that she works with Morvern in the Supermarket and that work-mates form the most common social bonding among the working-class citizens of the Port, and both graffiti highlight the sexual open-mindedness and experience of the two young women.

This is a few stages away from the way in which more toilet graffiti, and the rude signs the schoolgirls hold up to the back window of the bus, are represented in *The Sopranos*. Warner says, "I saw 'beware of limbo dancers' in a toilet once and just thought it was very funny, and of course, illustrations of the phallus have a rich art historical tradition going back to pre-history! In *Morvern*, the graffiti isn't rendered in facsimile like in *The Sopranos*—I guess I was too cautious, textually to do that at that stage." Nevertheless, the inclusion of Red Hanna's hand-drawn map for Lanna in *Morvern Callar* is along exactly the same lines as the scrawled comments in *The Sopranos* or the posters reproduced in *These Demented Lands*—all serve a curious double function. On the one hand they seem to reinforce a sense of realism, in that they appear to verify the fictional world described in the narrative by incorporating pieces of "evidence" of its existence into the text. However, their very qualities of apparent realism serve to remind the reader of the artificiality of the rest of the text, and thus to remind them that they are engaged in the supremely artificial act of reading. As Warner points out, when Morvern writes the postcard:

That's when you see Morvern actually write something down, before that she's written the priority stacking list of fresh fruit and veg at the Supermar-ket, again highlighted out from the block text and that's the irony of it— It's HER highlighting this by using capitals and separating it from the rest of the text, it's ALL her text, it's her novel in the first person!

The brevity of her message and its isolation from the rest of the text draws attention to the fact that this novel is narrated by a character who is deeply uncomfortable with communication and the written word, and also foregrounds the ways in which authorship is such a central theme in the book. The plot of *Morvern Callar* is determined by the fact that Morvern's boyfriend finished his novel and then killed himself—everything that Morvern does in the book follows from this. We never get to read his novel, but Morvern does submit it to the literary publisher of the dead boyfriend's choice, where it is immediately and enthusiastically accepted for publication. Crucially, this is the next text we see Morvern write on her boyfriend's computer, which she clearly knows how to use. She deletes his name from the disk and claims authorship for it herself.

BY MORVERN CALLAR. (p. 84)

This is a crucial dramatic moment in the novel, but despite all the latent drama of Morvern's situation and her disposal of a corpse, it is the empowerment of this act of writing these words that motivates the forward narrative of the novel.

The novel that we read (as opposed to the novel of which she is claiming authorship within the narrative) is written in her voice. As Warner says:

It's obsessed with texts. A story about someone who's never read a novel, who publishes a novel which she hasn't written, but who obviously has written a novel to explain these events, or, can I say to confess, cause what we see is her text, what she's written down, that's what we're reading, that's why we see these images—Red Hanna's map and so on. These are the textual imperatives that Morvern has chosen to highlight. You know it's all her text, it's strange, I once was talking to someone in the pub and she swore to me that *Morvern Callar* was written in the third person, she couldn't recall it was in the first; she had this sense that the story had been told to her in the third person. It's interesting that. I can think of books I read when I was young that still have left an impression on me, stuff by Hesse and Zweig, but I cannot recall the narrative method . . . sometimes it can be curiously invisible. I think, with *Morvern* what I was trying to do was to write a book which would never be published, so I wanted these nasty enormous ironies contained in the manuscript, so that when it was found—long after I'd hanged myself!—you could see the irony of the fact that it's an unpublished novel about someone who can't write a novel but who has had a novel published. But of course it all fell apart because it was published!!! I never had a hope in my mind of being published any more than I had one of winning jackpot in the lottery in those days, cause I so felt I was working without the realms of "correct usage," which I now just see as a mystifying obfuscation, held up as an ideal because it prevents whole worlds and experiences that would be uncomfortable to the artistic and political status quo from being rendered forth. Essentially, if we follow through these concepts of "correct usage", my lived experiences, and those of countless others, are being condemned as irrelevant and unsuitable as material for artistic expression. I just thought to hell with all that! Like when Picasso wanted to paint a newspaper but instead, just pasted one into the canvas with varnish. I'm not saying I'm a comparable artist with Picasso, but I think the beauty of any art form is its infinity . . . it will go on developing, changing, it won't be pinned down under glass and told to stay still. Everyone has their own taste, of course, if people feel the novel ended in the 19th Century and everything written since is by artistic pygmies, this is essentially a statement of personal taste, but that is different from inventing artistic rules that actively prevent the forward movement of the medium. Art will always surprise the status quo, by finding a way through, like water, all water is trapped water, it finds a way to flow onwards, to keep moving. Artistic conservatives want to freeze it.

Warner's obsession with textuality continued in *These Demented Lands,* which is divided into sections called "First Text," "Second Manuscript," and "The Letter" and includes occasional insertions, each with their own "Editor's note" stating that, for instance, a poster has been inserted into the manuscript, or a press release glued into it — both are reproduced in the novel. Warner has a particular affection for *These Demented Lands.* "It's my most literary novel and my favourite, though of course it's not my most popular, critically, but some strange young readers prefer it to Morvern! It was a real honour to dedicate it to Michael Ondaatje and Mark Richard who'd been so encouraging to me personally about Morvern at a time when I felt like giving up writing for silence."

Morvern finds the Aircrash Investigator's manuscript and reproduces a section of it in the beginning of her text, commenting approvingly on his use of language. This element of meta-narrative was originally going to be taken onto a whole new level in Warner's initial introduction to the novel, which was to have been based on the papers of the Outer Rim Bar Literary Debating Society, who were supposed to have found the manuscripts which form the body of the novel and to be discussing them. "These literary debating societies go on all over. I saw a poster advertising one for *Morvern Callar* in a local library just recently but I was too shy to turn up myself. Those societies are as valid in their conclusions as any bunch of savants at a Uni; more so I would say. I did sneak back later and take the poster for it though!" In the end Warner abandoned this framing device concept:

It was clever-clever and cluttering it up. When I came to edit the book down I just felt that the central manuscripts stood more mysteriously on their own. The debate stuff was making it into a much more explained book, so I abandoned that and left them as unedited texts. One day I might do a limited edition, full length version. You see Hardy and Conrad and that windbag James' collected works and there are all these added sections, expurgated chapters added to the original, like in *Jude the Obscure* or whatever. Or say Malcolm Lowry's many changes to the final text of *Aquamarine.* I don't see my novels as necessarily finished, I might change them at any moment! I find that quite exciting, the idea that the books are variable, are infinitely expandable.

MONEY, WORK, AND DEATH

There are many echoes of Victorian melodrama (bizarrely, given Warner's other influences) in *Morvern Callar*'s plot: a rootless orphan girl gets a sudden windfall from a mysterious benefactor and goes off to travel the world, returning pregnant and penniless, alone in a snowstorm. Morvern is insistent in the text on her rootlessness. She always refers to Red Hanna as her foster dad — although she shares his surname, she evidently doesn't feel the security of being adopted wholly into another family. She doesn't know which village her birth mother came from, or indeed anything else about her, while her foster mum is dead and evidently much missed. As is the case in many a Victorian potboiler, or indeed acknowledged masterpieces from *Jane Eyre* to almost all of Dickens, the book's story hinges on an impoverished orphan coming into money and dealing with the conseqences.

The impression given by many reviewers is that Warner writes about wild young women and popular culture, whereas the way he sees it,

All my books are about poverty, about people trying to get a few joys with not much in their pocket, and then they're about the moral vacuum when you have money. I see them firmly in an existential tradition. They get seen as books about young girls, but I see them as books about our lives — where do we go with our lives when we're going to die? I'm still led by Sartrean existentialism and absurdity, these philosophers I read when I was 16 or 17. It's interesting that the world of philosophy can be as fickle and fashionable as the literary world. Philosophy has moved on enormously but I'm still working through the implications of '50s existentialism because I don't think that's exhausted yet — I think I'm still grappling with those existential dilemmas!

The lack of money in the Port is not something Morvern ever explicitly discusses. It's too obvious for her to mention, just as she never points out that the sky is above the ground or that sunset happens once a day — poverty is a similar fact of life. However, it is indirectly alluded to throughout the novel — for instance, everyone Morvern encounters, not just Lanna but Creeping Jesus and Tequila Sheila, notice and comment upon her new jacket — Morvern turning up in a new and obviously expensive article of clothing is not an everyday event. Neither Morvern nor Lanna will cancel their holiday, despite their row, because having the money to go away is a one-off event, not a chance to be tossed aside easily. At the party near the beginning of the novel, which takes place in "a big bungalow" in the area outside the Port, where "only well-to-do live . . . in bought houses," Morvern is talking to an architecture student who asks her what kind of house she'd like — she says, "one where you couldn't hear the men go to the toilet" (p. 22). What she wants is space and privacy (which she gets in the end not by living in a big house but through her European travels). The accretion of these small details about living on not enough money goes alongside more politicized statements, such as Morvern's description of how she has ended up working full time at the superstore:

Cause of tallness I had started part-time with the superstore when thirteen, the year it got built. The superstore turn a blind eye; get as much out you as they can. You ruin your chances at school doing every evening and weekend. The manager has you working all hours, cash in hand, no insurance, so when fifteen or sixteen you go full-time at the start of that summer and never go back to school. (p. 10)

Or there is Morvern's casual equation of poverty with war:

then the Meals on Wheels arrived for Couris Jean. The woman driver told about how she couldnt get to some houses and about how some old folks couldnt afford heating. The big metal soup urn was in the open air and some snow was stuck to the bottom of it, as if poor people were in a war that no one else was. (34)

The master of the political speech within the text though is Morvern's foster father, Red Hanna, whose response to Morvern's comment that "there's still small pleasures" is:

But no big pleasures for the likes of us, eh? We who eat from the plate thats largely empty. I've saved for this early number, now it's coming I feel empty, the overtime has just gobbled up the years and heres you, twenty-one, a forty-hour week on slave wages for the rest of your life; even with the fortnight in a resort theres no much room for poetry there, eh?(p. 44)

He goes on to say that:

the hidden fact of our world is that theres no point in having desire unless youve money. Every desire is transformed into sour dreams. You get told if you work hard you get money but most work hard and end up with nothing. I wouldnt mind if it was shown as the lottery it is but oh no. The law as brute force has to be worshipped as virtue. Theres no freedom, no liberty; theres just money. (p. 45)

When writing the novel, Warner considered the idea that Morvern's relationship with her boyfriend might have been unhappy or abusive, or that Red Hanna might have abused her, but he decided against such slick solutions to the question as to what might have made her react in such a way to her boyfriend's death. Instead, the most immediate reason behind her coolness when faced with his dead body comes from the fact that her work in the supermarket has brutalized her—she is used to handling carcasses, and well used to the sight of blood. As Warner puts it, "once the body's dead it's become like the meat or the packages she daily hoiks in the super-market, so she goes on camping trips in the good weather to bury it." As Morvern describes it at the beginning of the novel, working in the meat section is a horrible experience:

I used to work in the meat. You cleaned up each night. Afterwards you smelled of blood and it was under your nails as you lifted the glass near your nose in the pub. You pulled the bleeding plastic bag of gubbins, cut open by bones, to the service lift. Blood spoiled three pairs of shoes. You were expected to supply your own footwear. (p. 12)

Even aside from the brutalities of the meat section, Morvern's working life is described as a series of small humiliations:

At the till I filled plastic carrier bags with Christmas stuff for folk. A woman with a well-to-do south voice told me to wash my soily hands before touching her messages. Some bills came to hundreds of pounds. They all paid with these credit cards. I put the bags in trolleys and pushed them to the Volvos. I had a well-to-do family and their voices. The biggest bill and a trolley just for wine. A daughter my age who looked on while I loaded the boot. No change for a tip cause they used credit card. The husband went, Merry Christmas. After service me and Smiler let the section run down but Creeping Jesus made us stock up just before the superstore shut so there would be tons to take off after the shoppers left though we werent paid a penny after closedown. (pp. 10–11)

Other small asides hinting at the unbearable quality of Morvern's working life are scattered throughout the text: "Don't talk about work Lanna, I cant face the thought of it tomorrow, I goes" (p. 103). Or, in the scene when Morvern moves her boyfriend's dead body up into the loft, we're told that the corpse is "heavier than a six-wheeler loaded with tatties" (p. 51). Equally telling is the repeated use of "as per usual" in connection with work, suggesting its utter tedium.

This aspect of the novel, the fact that it's about someone trying to escape from a mind-numbing, desensitizing job, has been ignored by most commentators, who also tend for similar reasons to miss the significance of Morvern's repeated naming of everything around her. Warner sees this as springing from her insecurity and the poverty of her childhood—naming gives power, and implies ownership, which is immensely important to Morvern. Money matters to her in a way which is alien to anyone who has never had to worry about how to stretch a tiny income in enough directions to cover the bare necessities. Her insistence on brand names, and her delight at her spending power on holiday both spring from this—and in her dealings with the London-based publishers, her relationship with money is thrown into sharp (and very funny) contrast with their incomprehension of how it is possible to lack money so absolutely.

Finally, there is the fact that this is a novel which opens with a still-bleeding corpse. Literary convention might make readers expect a whodunit, but since the very first sentence is "He'd cut His throat with the knife," that's obviously not going to be the case. Readers might still expect a whydunit instead—if so, they will be disappointed. We get his suicide note in the fullness of time, and learn from Lanna another reason why he might have been prompted to take his own life—but Morvern's focus as narrator is not on why her boyfriend chose to kill himself, but on how she's going to live with the consequences of his act.

GENDER

Warner's choice of a female narrator for his first novel (in contrast, for instance, to the early stories published by the Clocktower Press) was made partly in order to get away from the crippling myth of the macho male writer, the Hemingway or the Kerouac:

There was this huge romantic mythology about what a male writer was meant to be like, you know, you were meant to know famous people and I didn't, you were living in your garret with good cheap wine in Paris, dating aristocrats, big game-hunting, bull fighting and deep sea fishing with the odd civil war thrown in. I mean, like the University myth I believed you had to live this wild, dramatic life to become a writer! Funny really, the closest I'd get would be spying a fox and hooking a rainbow trout in the burn but it made me feel terribly inadequate and I think that autobiographical urge in writing is terribly damaging and probably, when I began to suss it was all a sham, helped by Beckett, it's something to do with why *Morvern Callar* was my first novel. It was a textual flight from that male first autobiographical novel. I am working on a book that's largely autobiographical but with *Callar* it was such a formal relief to work my way free of all that romantic stuff through the actual process of writing the prose. I mean I see myself as reacting against all that macho male writer autobiographical approach.

This gives a different spin on why *Morvern* is written in the first person — and why her boyfriend, who shares a number of biographical details with Warner (he is roughly the same age when he commits suicide as Warner was when he wrote the novel, both were brought up in hotels outside the real and imagined Oban, they share an obsession with trains, etc.), has to be killed off in the first line of the book. This takes the critical theory of the "Death of the author" to one of its possible extremes — kill off the autobiographical author figure and inhabit the voice of the Other, the female. "He" goes unnamed, in a novel which obsessively names everything else, perhaps because naming confers power and infers ownership, and despite Morvern's posthumous appropriation of her boyfriend's money and his novel, she knows the limitations of her power over him during his lifetime. The device of always referring to "Him" with an initial capital is deeply disturbing, increasing the sense of "His" power, by equating it with God's — the author of all creation.

Morvern's reactions, or more precisely, her lack of reaction to her boyfriend's death spring not only from the brutalization of her job, but also from the fact that she lives in a culture which is full of brutality, which Warner characterizes as male brutality against women. The novel is full of such anecdotes, such as a temporarily fostered girl from an abusive home, telling Morvern of how her father had repeatedly anally raped her, or Lanna's story about her brother-in-law pushing his pregnant wife's face into the scullery sink, then knocking her onto the floor and saying that "if the dishes had been done like a decent wife should, the water would have been deep enough to drown her properly" (p. 16). This is an aspect of the novel which even those critics preoccupied by the "man writes as woman" issue have not tended to pick up on — the fact that it describes a culture in which women are frequently victims, but whose heroine never sees herself as passive victim but instead casts herself in the role of agent of her own destiny, not only telling her own tale in the book that we read, but appropriating the male voice by presenting her boyfriend's novel as if it is her own. Even when critics have interpreted events as suggesting that Morvern is trapped by her own physicality, there are alternative readings. As Warner suggests, she retains her own agency throughout:

For instance, it's assumed Morvern "fell pregnant" (and doesn't that phrase tell us a lot about man made language?) but I actually think she could equally well have got pregnant by choice. However, the interpretations of her pregnancy have always been that she got pregnant unintentionally/ helplessly etc . . . in other words, critics' interpretations of the book have assumed she wasn't in control, but where is that stated?

In life, Morvern is taciturn and the female characters around her are abused or silenced, either by death, as in the case of her foster mother, or dumbness, as in the case of Couris Jean — but in the two novels, the one we read and the one we don't, women's voices are triumphant. However, since the "real" author of the book we read *is* male, we end up with gender complications on the scale of *Twelfth Night* — in this case, Warner is impersonating woman's voice, while within the text she is appropriating a male-authored novel.

While Warner has spoken of his relief at the positive response of most women to the book, there are those who have criticized his portrayal of women. The novelists Janice Galloway, Zoë Strachan, and A. L. Kennedy have all expressed reservations on this subject, Galloway saying:

Men adopting female personae are . . . writing women out of their heads, male interpretations of women. Male visions. How could they be anything else? Alan Warner's women for example. Never done fiddling with their stockings. Doesn't *invalidate* what else he's saying — of course not — but it does remind you Alan's doing the observing. Which he is. There's no invisible narrator — that's a fallacy. (*Edinburgh Review*, 1999, p. 94)

This comment was made in passing during a lengthy interview and was not intended to stand as a serious critique of Warner's writing, but it does articulate something referred to by several of Warner's readers, of both sexes — some are impressed at what they see as an uncanny ability to inhabit a female skin, and others see male voyeurism. Perhaps these two states are not, in any case, mutually exclusive — Lynne Ramsay, director of the film adaptation of the novel, spoke during an Edinburgh Film Festival interview in the summer of 2000 of how impressed she had been, overall, at Warner's ability to capture a convincing female voice, but how certain scenes, such as Lanna and Morvern taking a bath together, had smacked of male fantasy to her. Jenny Turner, one of the book's most perceptive critics, finds a way around this dichotomy. Describing Morvern's gift of beauty, and quoting Couris Jean's comment that her face is that of "an angel come down to this earth," Turner writes that:

Like the love she has known and the money she has come into, Morvern's beauty frees her from pointless want. Unlike a real-life woman, she does not paint her toenails or moisturise her body from an impulse based at bottom on insecurity, a sense that no matter how nice she looks, she can never look nice enough. Whatever she does with her body, she does it purely for pleasure and preening. This is a rigorous and self-aware fantasy projection. How can the male gaze ever intrude on an image of shameless, self-sufficient perfection? How can it be thought, come to that, to be intruding on an image entirely made by itself? (*LRB*, 2.11.95, p. 23)

Turner then goes on to echo the words of Morvern's boyfriend's suicide note to her, writing, "For Warner is of course everywhere in this story, in the corner of every room, at the edge of every word." In Turner's reading of the novel, Morvern is "an earth-bound angel . . . a poetic image." She writes that, "In the shape of [Morvern's] own face unpeeled as a face-pack she finds an image of Platonic infinity, the unfolding of form on form." For Turner, the fact that Morvern is a male-created Goddess figure is not a flaw in the novel, but is among its greatest achievements. She writes that:

For the author, there is the sublime impossibility of ever fusing with this woman he has created. For the reader, there is the confusion even of knowing who it is precisely that you want to fuse with: the author who has concealed himself so cleverly? The fictional construct whom we have come to know so well? Again, this puzzlement only makes explicit the reader's relationship to all narrators. It is when you come closest to touching them that you most painfully realise that they're only shapes made out of words.

Whereas, for Turner, Warner's Venus/angel figure is too self-contained and elusive to be intruded upon by the male gaze, Zoë Strachan has a different response to the suggestion of voyeurism. In her essay "Queerspotting," which looks at homosexuality in the fictions of Irvine Welsh and Alan Warner, she writes that:

the strong homoerotic subtext between Morvern and her best friend Lanna is played out in a series of rather exploitative scenes. In some cases a male character is present to assume the role of voyeur, at other times it is left up to the reader to do so. For example, Lanna tends to help Morvern to get changed, always "biting her lip," apparently an indication of scarcely concealed lust. When Morvern puts on her supermarket uniform, Lanna, "smoothed the nylon onto me with her palms." Lanna also fastens Morvern's suspenders before a night out, then later on unrolls Morvern's stockings to reveal her glittery knee to the men in the pub. "Everyone was watching," and some men whistle at her exposed thigh. When they finally end up at a party, they decide, somewhat bizarrely, to have a shower together, "as per usual . . . to save time." This (naturally) allows plenty of opportunity for soaping each other and so on. It is hardly a surprise when at the end of the night a game of strip poker turns into a menage à quatre. At first Morvern just watches, but soon she joins in as well, "I let them do anything to me and tried to make each as satisfied as I could." (*www.spikemagazine.com/0599queerspotting.htm*)

For Strachan, the element of voyeurism is inextricably caught up in a male girl-on-girl fantasy, although this is never fully developed in the novel. Strachan is more interested in the portrayal of lesbian desire in *The Sopranos*, although she points out even there that the characters are unwilling to label themselves as lesbian, and there is a sense that Fionnula and Kay are, as Kay describes Catriona "just that bit bi." While there is no reason why a female narrator should not express desire for another female character, or as in the case of Morvern and Lanna, simply seem sensually aware of one another, Strachan, like Lynne Ramsay and Janice Galloway, is skeptical that anything more complex or subversive than the male gaze is being conveyed here. Of course, male voyeurism is itself something of a theme in the book — not only in the scenes of Morvern and Lanna together, but also in asides such as Morvern's mention of "one young husband owned a camcorder so his four married brothers and him swapped porno videos of their unknowing wives" (p. 43). However, Warner himself, while not denying the suggestion of male voyeurism, suggests that there is both a "realistic" justification for Morvern and Lanna's central bathing together scene in Couris Jean's flat, and an increase in dramatic intensity — and he also points out that, for all Lynne Ramsay's reservations, this scene was always included in every one of the filmscript's many incarnations. The justification for this scene at the level of realism is that Morvern and Lanna have a bath together because they are freezing after their scantily clad walk through the snow back from the party and there's only enough hot water for one bath full, as was the case in Oban council houses, without waiting an hour for the immerser to heat the water. As for dramatic tension, Warner feels that:

If you think about it, because they are *facing* one another it made Morvern's dialogue "He's gone away" and Lanna's interrogation of her seem more intense to me, because their eyes and gaze are forced directly *at* each other and it's harder for Morvern to lie, being physically right up next to Lanna, knees knocking together. I don't think that's a sexy scene at all. I think it's sweet when they shampoo each other's hair for a moment and fling shampoo at each other. It's only thought sexy because they whisper about the sex with the guys in the past tense. People are such *prudes*. So despite my bath fetish there are purely dramatic benefits from that scene

This argument seems a strong one for this scene, although for those for whom male voyeurism is an issue, it leaves open the question as to quite why Morvern and Lanna need to shower and swim naked together *quite* so often during the rest of the book.

A. L. Kennedy's comments when asked in an interview about men writing as women, and specifically about *Morvern Callar*, also chime with a sense of Morvern as the projection of a male fantasy, but she also finds some of her language unconvincing:

I didn't know about *Morvern Callar*, some of the things . . . I've spoken to guys about it and some guys as well went "Eh — I don't think so." Slightly more about wish fulfillment I think. But the whole thing about how you must always wipe your bum in a particular direction, it's like, "Ah, you got that out of a medical textbook, I'm sorry." (*Edinburgh Review*, 1999, pp. 114–5)

Warner has responded that this phrase, and others such as Morvern's remarks about her "oily T-Zone," were lifted directly from women's magazines, and that he feels it's part of Morvern's narrative style to quote, magpie-like, from other sources — another example would be the phrase "you were expected to supply your own footwear" (p. 12) in the description of working in the meat section, which is obviously an echo of a training manual. However, a strong case could be argued in support of A. L. Kennedy's view here. The magazine-style phrases sit quite awkwardly within Morvern's discourse, appearing *too* self-conscious. Women tend to be so immersed in this kind of language that it becomes more diffused into their own speech, so it seems unconvincing to find sudden phrases dropped into Morvern's narrative like small bombs. There are times when Warner seems seduced by the poetic qualities of the trappings of femininity — Morvern always refers to her lipsticks or nail varnishes by the manufacturers' shade descriptions: "dusky cherry" and so on. Based on purely personal and anecdotal evidence, it could be said that few women refer to their lipsticks by the names allotted them by the cosmetics companies, instead they tend to say "the pinkier one" or "the bright red one" or "the one that goes with my top"—lending some weight to Kennedy's sense of an artificially constructed description of femininity. However, these are small carpings balanced against the very real power of Morvern's elusive but distinctive voice.

Of course, the aspect of femininity most obviously skirted around in the novel is that of motherhood. Morvern refers constantly to Mull as the island where her foster mother is buried. Wherever she goes in the Port, she glimpses the Island—she's constantly confronted by her fostermother's absence. She knows nothing about where her biological mother comes from, and is even apparently unaware as to whether she is alive or dead; and she despises Vanessa "the Depresser," Red Hanna's girlfriend and thus a potential replacement mother-figure (who is in any case supplanted by Lanna); and finally, Lanna's grandmother, Couris Jean, the only positive maternal figure in the book, dies while Morvern is in Spain. This may lie behind Morvern's fascination with the "virgin saint girl," whose statue is carried in procession through the village in Spain to the fishermen's church, with young girl's hands reaching out to touch it, before it is ritually burned at sea. Morvern, along with other young girls, swims out at dawn "trying to see her burned face looking up at us from the seabed below" (p. 156). Since the statue is, if not the Virgin Mary, then clearly a symbol of renewal, rebirth, and fertility for the community, Morvern's dawn communion with her and the young girls suggests a longing for the maternal, both a mourning for her own mother(s) and an intimation of her own motherhood, yet to come in the book's story. This lends more weight to War-

ner's suggestion that Morvern's pregnancy is a deliberate choice —
a desire to become the mother she has lacked herself.

POPULAR CULTURE

Warner is frustrated by the tendency of academics to put him and
his work in a box marked "popular culture," but his novels do pay
tribute to the branding of signs on the consciousness of their characters. The Swedish translation of *Morvern Callar* emphasizes this,
the book shaped to look like a pack of Silk Cuts, its inside covers
printed over and over with the road sign, all of which goes to
emphasize the fact that Morvern's world is made up not of books,
which she scarcely mentions, but visual signs, which permeate her
narrative — she never fails to tell the reader the brand of cigarettes
she is smoking, or what the tracks are on the tape to which she is
listening. Strikingly, Warner's novels find a significant part of their
readership among people who wouldn't normally read books — as
an author he is unusual in combining prize-winning critical success
with high sales figures and an identification with a distinctly non-
literary audience — "it's nice when young people buy your books
too, and people who don't normally read books. I get a lot of letters
too, which is so much more lovely than getting reviews." Warner
objects quite reasonably to the one-track mind of those in the media
who represent writers such as himself, Irvine Welsh, Gordon Legge,
or Laura Hird as part of the "disco biscuits generation" and who
can't seem to see beyond an identification with rave music. As he
points out, in *Morvern Callar* Morvern listens to all sorts of music,
and rave is scarcely mentioned in *The Sopranos*, but interviews such
as those in the new Canongate collection (entitled, as if in reference
to Warner's frustration, *The Repetitive Beat Generation*) ignore all

other musical references, let alone the influence of other writers, or philosophy, or the visual arts. As he says:

I'm suspicious of the idea that certain types of music have been zeroed in on just because the dominant culture is ruled by 35 year-old men like myself who found a little escapism in that scene. . . . go talk to 15 year-old kids about rave, that's interesting, but 35 year-old men idolising it is boring — just because they got a last blast of adolescence with an ecky tab down them. . . . I just think it's all sad — it all happened for me in the late '80s, then it all got commercialised and I got bored. People will insist on banging on about it.

The musical influence which *does* interest him with regard to his own work is that of Holger Czukay, with whom he is collaborating on writing a book, which he sees as the best way to pay Czukay back for what he's learned from his music. He sees Czukay as exemplary of an artistic tradition of mastering styles and then reject- ing them and moving on (he also cites Picasso's comment that to imitate other artists is understandable but to imitate yourself is pathetic) — in Czukay's case this includes starting as a classically trained musician then moving from classical music to the atonal music of the 1960s, then to the formation of the rock group The Can, with whom he played for ten years before moving on yet again, abandoning traditional instruments, experimenting with tape recorders and precursors to sampling. Warner is much taken with this credo of restriction as the mother of invention, the idea that this forces you into a powerful creativity. He suggests that he sees his own talents as restricted and was therefore pleased with the notion that he could make a virtue of his own limitations and see them as the source of creative power.

The desire to lump his generation of Scottish writers as a "beat generation" following in the footsteps of Kerouac and others leaves Warner mystified:

I've read two Kerouac novels, one Burroughs and Ginsberg's *Howl* and I don't feel influenced by them at all—nor am I even particularly interested in them. My reading in American fiction started with Dos Passos and Scott Fitzgerald and Hemingway, and moved from there to Pynchon, Mailer, and onwards to Marc Richard and Annie Proulx—this vision of us as "the beats, driving in our tartan minibus to Inverness" was used without any reference to the texts. *On the Road* was a crap novel—Kerouac's whole style was flawed because it had to include everything, including the dross, and I think his work was a tragic failure—and Burroughs can take as many drugs as he wants, he'll never be as radical as Beckett. I think it's obvious that I'm not influenced by any of it.

LANDSCAPE AND MYTH

In the course of our interview, Warner described "figures moving across landscapes" as becoming more of a theme in his books, and this can indeed be seen starting in Morvern's journey into the hills to bury the body of her dead lover followed by her attempts to find sanctuary both in Spain and, in *These Demented Lands*, on the Island. The sopranos too travel across Scotland and back in the course of a day, while *The Man Who Walks* is entirely structured around an epic pursuit round the Highlands, but the journeys in the novels he hasn't yet published are greater in scope, both geographically and chronologically. One of his long-standing, but as yet unpublished projects, *The Permanent Way*, a novel set largely on the railways, covers ten or twelve years over the course of its plot, and its central character is based on a version of Warner himself, if he hadn't left Oban and his job working on the railways to go off to university and ultimately become a writer. Landscape is explored particularly through another of the central characters, who is a geologist, and thus has a different perspective on both place and time, and her job of planning the burial of toxic waste in the

Highlands for a large chemical firm draws attention (as do the nuclear submarines which cruise offshore from the Port in *The Sopranos*) to the dangers hidden just beneath the beautiful surface of the Highlands landscape. *Black Lochs*, by contrast (also unpublished), is a historical novel, set in the aftermath of Waterloo, its genesis coming from Warner's astonishment at discovering that the victorious soldiers, far from being showered with medals and money and given a hero's welcome, were abandoned after the battle and had to work at whatever employment they could find to earn the money to make their ways back home again. The novel concerns two soldiers of the Black Watch Regiment and the two years it takes them to work their way north through England and the southern and central belts of Scotland to their homes in the Highlands, working as farm laborers and, at one stage, in an ice house. Warner is clearly fascinated by a period he describes as "surreal . . . people had wooden false teeth and women used straw as tampax . . . you don't need to be florid and over the top, it's just mad times." Epic journeys also drive the plot of an as-yet untitled novel (provisionally called either *Oscillator* or *Follana*, after its protagonist) — the two central characters are a Spanish businessman tracking down his ex-lovers across Europe, and his Sancho Panchez-like sidekick, an economic refugee from sub-Saharan Africa, who has made a perilous and life-changing journey just to reach Spain in the first place. It was Warner's parents' journeys across war-torn Europe — his father (from Sheffield) who joined up to fight in the World War II, and his mother (from the Isle of Mull), who joined up as an ambulance driver — which caused them to meet and marry, while spending the first three years of their lives together working to find homes for refugees. The earliest stories Warner can remember hearing concern rootless people, trying to make their way home across Europe, a factor which seems to be influencing the patterns of the stories he himself tells now.

In *Morvern Callar* there are, as the critic Jenny Turner points out, three separate landscapes which echo one another, and which she describes as:

a village bounded on the one side by mountains and on the other by the sea, with a couple of council estates, a couple of bars, and then some richer houses and a big hotel as you move out and up the road. Sometimes the village is the damp and downtrodden Scottish port; sometimes it's a blazing hot and glorious Balearic resort. And sometimes it's the boyfriend's model railway, with the corpse of a man laid out on it, like Gulliver. (*LRB*, 2.11.95, p. 23)

Many critics have commented on the "timeless" nature of the landscape described in all Warner's novels, and its contrast with the depiction of the details of day-to-day normality (eyeshadow, Diet Coke, etc.). There is very much a sense in *Morvern Callar* that the landscape around the Port and in Spain is immeasurably ancient — when Morvern is on one of her camping trips in the mountains, she comments that "I looked out at the landscape moving without haste to no bidding atall" (p. 90). In the night swimming sequence in Spain, Morvern describes how, as she swims out to sea, "you couldnt see the lights of the restaurants, only moon above the sharp cliffs and moon splattered across the sea I was in" (p. 208). As she leaves the temporal world of restaurants behind her, her use of "moon" without the definite article increases the sense of timelessness, and even myth — it's not "the moon," which can be defined and pinned down, but simply "moon," too powerful for analysis. She continues, "All was made of darknesses," a phrase which contains Biblical echoes of the creation of the world in Genesis, and then "Stars were dished up all across bluey nighttimeness." As ever, for Morvern, color is indeterminate, *bluey*, and rather than a single night, she is describing "nighttimeness" as an eternal state of being (which can be switched on in the boyfriend's recreation of his home village, where "the tiny Tree Church flowered as per usual cause of the always summerness of the model village" (p. 51)). Next, Morvern writes:

I let my legs sink down; my nudeness below in the blackwater; legs hung in that huge deep under me and the layer on layer and fuzzy mush of star pinpricks were above with the little buzz of me in between. (p. 208)

The sea is unmeasurable, "that huge deep" and Morvern herself is at once acutely physically present, and unimaginably tiny, "the little buzz of me" suspended between the depth of the ocean and the space of the sky. No wonder that, when she returns to the shore, dresses and heads for the hotel, there is the sense that she's coming back from a huge journey.

This sense of a timeless landscape, along with Morvern's quality of being outside the law, and thus in some ways not constrained by the normal "rules" of human social behavior, may tie in with Warner's desire to make her in some ways a mythical figure:

There's a fashionable word in seventies criticism — "mythopoetic" — I always liked that word, and in *Morvern Callar* I wanted to tell a working class person's story as if it wasn't just realism, so that it had something of the quality of myth. In everything I've done, I wanted to try and give the impermanent the quality of myth — it's not enough to say "here's Joe Bloggs, he works on the railways and reads Chaucer," you need to make that mythical in some way, and that's not easy.

There are mythical scenes in *Morvern Callar* — the horses swimming up the beach to Couris Jean, the virgin and candles in the procession Morvern watches in Spain. Obviously, there's something mythical in what Morvern's done, dismembering and burying a

corpse in the hills. Even her characteristic quietness is seen by
Warner as having a mythic, fated quality to it, "because she's naturally silent and doesn't talk much, by her own nature, like in tragedy, she determines the nature of her own tragedy." As mentioned
in the section on gender above, the critic Jenny Turner sees Morvern as a semi-mythic angelic/goddess idealized female figure. It
would be possible to see a contradiction between the mythic qualities of the novel and its details of everyday life, which many critics
have seen as fitting snugly into a school of Scottish working-class
"gritty realism," but the example of folk tales or, even more specifically Scottish, ballads, suggests a serious precedent for the conjunction of the details of working-class life with a mythic, or even
fantastic element.

3

The Novel's Reception

BRITISH AND AMERICAN REVIEWS

When the Jonathan Cape original paperback of *Morvern Callar* came out at the beginning of 1995, it was treated as a serious literary debut and reviewed in the broadsheet newspapers as well as in *The London Review of Books* and *The Times Literary Supplement*. Many reviewers seem slightly unsure what to make of the book, shocked by its brutal subject matter and unusual heroine, but with some exceptions they tend to be impressed by the quality of the writing. Andrew Biswell's opening paragraph to his review in *The Times Literary Supplement* perhaps sums this up:

A novelist who kills his principal male character on the first page and has the heroine stub out her cigarette in a pool of his blood on page three is hardly unwilling to take chances. Alan Warner delivers nasty surprises like these on almost every page of his first novel, *Morvern Callar*, but he writes with enough excitement and confidence to get away with including some

episodes which would seem excessive if they were handled with less pa-
nache. (*TLS*, 31.3.95)

Not everyone agreed with this assessment. Brian Morton's review in
The New Statesman (which, incidentally, is littered with inaccura-
cies about the novel's plot, some of which suggest that he can't
possibly have read the whole book) suggests that Morvern is "an
unhappy, even misogynistic creation" and that:

The unhappiness of her life is readily detectable in the awkwardness of her
language. She speaks in bland pidgin — no f-words — that may very well be
an adequate interiorisation of her spiritual state, but sits awkwardly on the
page, the repetition of "silentness" for "silence" suggests unease rather than
anything more profound. (*New Statesman*, 10.3.95)

However, Jenny Turner in *The London Review of Books* compares
the novel to *The Great Gatsby*:

The same effortless surface, with an immaculate craft going on underneath.
The same bold, lucid use of outrageously gilded images, worked into the
texture of an otherwise quiet prose. The same structural ambivalence. All
of which are just pretentious ways of trying to say something like: you'll
whizz through it like a hot knife through butter, but I've read it several
times and I still can't pin it down. (*LRB*, 2.11.95, p. 23)

On the whole, the critics in Britain joined Turner in praising the
novel, while tending to find it rather an unnerving read, with Eliz-
abeth Young writing in *The Guardian* that "Morvern gleams like an
onyx from a vivid, macabre and lyrical book . . . she is impossible to
forget." (*The Guardian*, 21.2.95).

Warner's fellow novelists also praised the book. Along with Irvine
Welsh's comments on the back blurb of the Vintage edition is Nick
Hornby's statement that *Morvern* is "haunting and brilliantly origi-

nal," while the American novelist Marc Richard has described it as, "a wonder and a danger, not for the faint-hearted; the reader is cut open by a . . . saw finely sharpened on a stone of nihilism."

American critics have been no more able to agree with one another than their British counterparts. In the *New York Times Book Review*, Jennifer Kornreich describes Morvern as an "apathetic delinquent" suffering from an "emotional anesthesia" which nothing can penetrate, and she thinks that the novel is permeated with "jaded resignation." She writes that, "while Morvern's opacity is obviously meant to convey hip disaffection, the novel's matter-of-fact amorality quickly grows tiresome" (*NYTBR*, 18.5.97). However, in *Salon*, Charles Taylor also feels an unease about Morvern's perceived "hipness" but considers the novel to be "the best of the new Scottish writing" and writes that, "Morvern is engaging, determined to express what she can't quite articulate, and Warner is a compelling storyteller." (*www.salon.com/april97/sneaks/sneak970417*)

POPULAR NON-CRITICAL SUCCESS

The fact that *Morvern Callar* was perceived to be selling to "non-readers" (i.e., the youth market which traditional publishers had long since given up trying to reach) influenced the marketing campaigns for the subsequent anthologies which also featured Warner's work—although it should be emphasized that the presence of writing by Irvine Welsh in the anthologies was considered, in the wake of the phenomenal success of the film of *Trainspotting*, to be the "crunch" factor. As will be discussed in the next section, on the marketing of the book, *Morvern Callar*'s publishers did not explicitly set out to tap into this non-traditional market, but the novel seems to have reached these readers by word of mouth. Clues to the people perceived to be reading the novel can therefore be picked up by looking at the marketing campaigns for the anthologies. In 1996, the year after *Morvern Callar* first came out, Rebel Inc. (an imprint of the Edinburgh publishers Canongate) published the anthology *Children of Albion Rovers*. Its editor, Kevin Williamson, used the conceit of a football team, with a "Team Talk" in place of introduction, and a "line up" including "an international keeper," Irvine Welsh, and Alan Warner as "a defender of the faith." The book was marketed with "football cards" of the authors and a huge nightclub launch. The inspiration behind this populist approach was the publishers' conviction that these were writers who were reaching an audience previously untapped by "literary fiction."

Sarah Champion, editor of the 1997 Sceptre anthology *Disco Biscuits*, describes in an interview with Steve Redhead, how, having decided to compile an anthology of writing about the dance scene, featuring work by Irvine Welsh, Jeff Noon, and Alan Warner, she conceived the marketing for that book, which was directly targeted at non-traditional book buyers:

I knew absolutely nothing about publishing whatsoever. But I think that was a big advantage. Because I just broke all the rules by not knowing that there were any. I decided what I wanted on the cover and told them all the "underground" dance magazines to send copies to, to get reviewed in . . . I automatically thought there should be a soundtrack CD . . . Also, I just automatically assumed there should be flyers . . . it worked — it actually reached people who probably wouldn't have just walked into a bookshop . . .

Disco Biscuits was just a one-off. The advance was £5,000 split between everybody. It was only supposed to sell 7,000 copies. It sold 60,000! But it sold almost all of these in the first six months in 1997. . . . I don't know who said it now but someone had said "surely people who go clubbing don't read." I can't remember where it came from but there was that general assumption and I think its partly to do with the fact that electronic music doesn't have words and therefore it can't be "intelligent." It did prove that people do read and they want books they can relate to. (Redhead, 2000)

Of course, the appropriation of the originally underground rave culture to make fast-turnaround best-selling anthologies such as *Disco Biscuits* and its sequel, *Disco 2000* (to which Warner did not contribute), which made healthy profits for a multinational media conglomerate, fits rather neatly with the Marxist critic Frederic Jameson's theory that capitalism revitalizes itself by absorbing all cultural production and making art into just another subsidiary of the market.

The fact that *Morvern Callar* was regularly described as "the first rave novel" meant that Alan Warner was much in demand for interviews and features outwith the literary press and in the pages of style magazines such as *The Face*, *GQ*, or *i-D*, which brought the book to the attention of yet more potential readers who would not necessarily normally read the books pages in the broadsheets or watch arts programs on television.

4

The Novel's Performance

MARKETING STRATEGY

Morvern Callar has sold 50,000 copies in Cape and Vintage paperbacks in Britain and 20,000 copies in the United States, and can expect to sell many more once the film adaptation has had its effect. From the beginning, the book was received as part of the rather ridiculous phenomenon memorably summed up in the style magazine headline "Is Scot Lit the new Brit Pop?" Those readers who had already come across Warner before reading his first novel would have done so in the context of the other writers published by Duncan McLean's Clocktower Press, such as Irvine Welsh, Gordon Legge, and Janice Galloway.

When the Jonathan Cape original paperback of *Morvern Callar* first came out in 1995, the blurb on the back cover suggested an attempt to have things both ways as regards the *Trainspotting* effect. The second paragraph describing the book runs as follows:

Moving from the rural poverty and drunken mayhem of the port to the tripped-out Mediterranean rave scene, we experience everything from Morvern's opaque, compelling perspective. Brutal, erotic and rich in a blood-dark humour, *Morvern Callar* is an enormously powerful debut. Using the voice of a young female narrator, Alan Warner's novel shifts the focus away from the male-dominated urban realism of much contemporary fiction and marks the arrival of a startling new Scottish writer.

Given that the purpose of a book's back cover blurb is to entice a potential reader to buy the book, this puts quite a dark interpretation on the novel, highlighting its concern with "rural poverty" and describing it as "opaque . . . brutal . . . blood-dark," although it does of course mention the more marketable qualities of eroticism and humor. The final sentence is particularly interesting with regard to the *Trainspotting* effect—emphasizing that this is a novel written in "the voice of a young female narrator" and explicitly disassociating it from "the male-dominated urban realism of much contemporary fiction", such as, one imagines, *Trainspotting* itself. However, Warner is described specifically as a Scottish, not British, writer, and the book's setting is described in the first line of the book's blurb as being "a remote Highland sea-port," so it is the urban, male-centerd nature of *Trainspotting* (and of course other English, male urban fictions such as those springing from the pens of Martin Amis and Will Self) from which *Morvern Callar* is being distanced, not its Scottishness. In any case, this care to disassociate the novel from the popular associations conjured up by *Trainspotting* in the blurb description is almost entirely undercut by what follows this para-graph—a large quote by Irvine Welsh. This is all the more signifi-cant for appearing on the cover of the first edition of the novel, since it is not a review of a published work already in the public domain, as are the reviews which plaster the mass-market Vintage paperback which came out the following year. Instead, it is a comment which readers will know has to have been made on the unpublished manuscript, suggesting a particular closeness between these two writers. The massively successful film of *Trainspotting* had not yet come out; the novel at this stage was still perceived as a cult, underground success and had not yet gone mainstream, nor had Irvine Welsh yet achieved notoriety for his endless generosity in blurbing other people's books; so all in all, using Welsh's name to help sell the book had slightly different connotations in 1995 to those it would have now. Also, in comparison with the manner in which the Edinburgh-based publishers Canongate/Rebel Inc. went on the following year to promote the anthology *Children of Albion Rovers* (discussed in the section "Popular Non-critical Success" above), the "Tartan Beat" aspect to *Morvern Callar*'s marketing was extremely subdued. However, Welsh's comment further undercuts the sober reading of the book in the paragraph quoted above, running as follows:

Morvern is a brilliant creation; a fearlessly cool and sassy party chick propelled by her own delicious morality around the geographic peripheries and fun epicentres of Europe. This piece of vital, European soul is more than a stunning debut novel; to my mind it establishes Alan Warner as one of the most talented, original and interesting voices around.

Those potential readers who might have been put off the notion of reading a "brutal" novel with an "opaque" narrator may instead be lured by the notion of reading about a "fearlessly cool and sassy party chick" who does not remain mired in Highlands poverty but makes her way around the "fun epicentres of Europe." However, the changes made for the mass-market Vintage paperback blurb are interesting in this context. The second paragraph of the blurb, quoted above, has disappeared to make way for the large numbers of quotes — and the "cool and sassy party chick" section of Welsh's

quote has also been cut. The understated monochrome front cover
of the Cape original has been replaced by a much brighter image,
which actually ties in more closely with the "party chick" angle,
which has been cut from the promotional text. The quote chosen
for most prominence, on the front cover, compares the book not to
Trainspotting, but to the English and American writers Ian McEwan
and Jay McInerney. Most striking, however, is the continued contrast with the manner in which the later anthologies *Disco Biscuits*
and *Children of Albion Rovers* were marketed. Warner's editor at
Cape, the hugely influential Robin Robertson (who also edits Irvine
Welsh, Gordon Legge, Duncan McLean, Janice Galloway, and
A.L. Kennedy), has said that neither he nor Reed Consumer Books
(which then owned the imprint, prior to its absorption in the Ran-
dom House conglomerate) expected huge commercial success from
Morvern Callar, or indeed any of the books by the above-mentioned
authors. As he says:

It's worth remembering that these books I worked on in the middle years
of the 90s were—in publishing terms—running completely against the
grain: each one regarded as a fresh commercial folly. I had support from
Dan Franklin, my boss then and now, but little or no help from the rest of
Reed Consumer Books. You can imagine how I feel about the bandwagon-
jumpers and their anthologies.[2]

Several of the anthologies which came out subsequent to the
success of *Trainspotting* and *Morvern Callar* seem to be based on a
one-dimensional misrepresentation of both Welsh's and Warner's
writing as simply celebrating popular or youth culture. But for
Morvern, far from being marketed as part of a mass music–based
phenomenon, Robertson's recollection is that,

As to publicity and marketing: well, we did all the usual things and I
remember sending out a lot of proofs to writers. The book did end up in

music stores, but that was their decision—we can't tell people to stock books.

In other words, *Morvern Callar* was treated not as a marketing opportunity, but as an exceptionally impressive literary debut—the media madness followed from a separate momentum, much of it generated by the international success of *Trainspotting* the film.

When I asked Warner about how he had felt about his books being presented by the media alongside Welsh's, his response was that he felt that they were very different writers and that this had been somewhat lost in the press hype. He has also felt frustrated on Welsh's behalf that the text itself was getting lost in the public perception of *Trainspotting*, the book as being just one element in the movie, the soundtrack, the poster, the T-shirt and so on, and its early pre-movie huge success as an underground word-of-mouth sales phenomenon seemed to be forgotten almost instantaneously:

On one level the success was fantastic but it has obscured things. Irvine and I are linked in the public eye with A.L. Kennedy, Gordon Legge and Duncan McLean but the links with poets such as Don Paterson, Roddy Lumsden, John Burnside, Robin Robertson and prose writers such as James Meek have been ignored. Also the influences of Jim Kelman, Edwin Morgan and perhaps even more strongly, Tom Leonard, have been minimised by journalists. The media wanted us to be a big gang, but they didn't want the poets to be included in the group.

While Warner enjoyed the success, he felt much less comfortable with the media's desire to create a Scot Lit scene, with, for instance the group photograph by Richard Avedon in the *New Yorker*:

The media wanted to portray a set of mindless ravers. The texts were dissolved and reified into covers and glossy magazine features. Duncan McLean was portrayed as having been influenced by *Trainspotting* and the fact that *Bucket of Tongues* and *Morvern Callar* had both been written *before Trainspotting* was something that journalists just couldn't seem to grasp. The frustrating thing was seeing great books like Ron Butlin's *The Sound of My Voice* or James Meek's fabulous *Drivetime* being ignored by the media, since they weren't seen as fitting in with the hype.

Peter Kravitz, in the introduction to the Picador anthology of contemporary Scottish writing, compares the Avedon photograph with Alexander Moffat's painting *Poet's Pub* (which hangs in the Scottish National Portrait Gallery) in which three pubs, Milne's Bar, The Abbotsford, and the Cafe Royal, are merged into one:

[Moffat] put MacDiarmid in the middle of a single canvas with Iain Crichton Smith, George Mackay Brown, Edwin Morgan, Sorley MacLean, Norman MacCaig and Robert Garioch. In hindsight this mythic combination marked the end of an era when poetry eclipsed prose, Edinburgh lorded it over Glasgow and women were left outside the pub of Scottish literature. The idea that you could fit Scotland's best writers round one table is inconceivable now. Yet a sincere attempt was made in 1995 when the *New Yorker* sent Richard Avedon to Glasgow to capture Scotland's best in a single posed team shot at the Clutha Vaults, a pub in the East End of Glasgow. In the sixteen years between Moffat's painting and Avedon's photograph the public landscape of Scottish writing has changed beyond recognition.

A few months later the *New York Times* magazine had a reporter set up a similar scene in Robbie's Bar in Leith. The piece appeared with the headline "The Beats of Edinburgh" and the sub-headline "from the margins of Scottish society comes a new, beer-soaked, drug-filled, profanity-laced, violently funny literature." (Kravitz, 1997, p. xxix)

This is precisely the kind of journalistic labeling which Warner, in common with all the other writers affected by it, finds both misleading and intensely frustrating, but the allure of "tartan beats" as a soundbite for journalists suggests that it will be some time before it goes away.

FILM INTEREST

From the moment it was first published, critics were commenting on *Morvern Callar's* filmic qualities — hardly surprising, since its construction (generally short scenes, with some flashbacks), the large amount of dialogue, the ready-made soundtrack presented by Morvern's obsessive detailing of track listings, the emphasis on landscape, Morvern's "close-up" attention to visual details, and the dramatic events of the plot all conspired to make it seem ideal for adaptation. On top of all this, once the *Trainspotting* film had made its huge impact on the scene — producers everywhere were suddenly actively looking for Scottish novels with references to drugs and popular culture. The BBC expressed interest in adapting the book almost immediately on its publication (and thus even before the film of *Trainspotting* had come out), but it wasn't until Hollywood came calling and bought the rights to *The Sopranos* that serious budgets started being discussed for *Morvern Callar.* Lynne Ramsay, who had won multiple awards for her first feature, the dreamy, lyrical but brutally unsentimental and altogether unsettling *Ratcatcher,* was brought in to direct, with the previously Oscar-nominated (for her role in Woody Allen's *Sweet and Lowdown*) young British actress Samantha Morton cast in the title role. One major change between the book and the novel is that Samantha Morton plays Morvern in her own (Nottingham) accent, further emphasizing her rootlessness and disconnection to the society she lives in. At the time of writing, the film is in post-production and is being subtitled in French in preparation for its launch at Cannes

Film Festival in 2002. The novel was adapted for screen by Lynne Ramsay in collaboration with Liana Dognini, with a significant level of input from Warner himself, who was also present for some of the filming, on location in and around Oban. He was extremely impressed by Samantha Morton's performance, describing his sense that as she walked on set and in front of a camera, he could see her transform herself into the character he had imagined on the page.

TREND-SETTING IMPACT?

The marketing of the 1996 anthology *The Children of Albion Rovers*, featuring writing by Irvine Welsh, Laura Hird, Alan Warner, and others, has been discussed above, but it was just one of a number of anthologies published in the late 1990s which either featured Warner's writing (as did Sarah Champion's *Disco biscuits: New fiction from the chemical generation*, which came out in 1997) or simply picked up on the drugs/music connotations which had been seized upon in Warner's writing by the media. Of all the possible trends for his writing to have set, this is probably the one which disturbs Warner himself the most. In recent years he has grown wary of appearing in anthologies at all and has done all within his power to distance his writing from the rave tag it acquired when *Morvern Callar* first came out.

More positively, the success of all Warner's novels has been one factor in helping to convince London-based publishers (most notably Jonathan Cape, Warner's own publisher) to take a risk and stray away from Anglo-centric, metropolitan fictions and to publish books by Scottish writers. It is by no means certain that writers such as Ali Smith (recently short-listed for the Booker Prize for her second novel, *Hotel World*) or Gordon Legge (recent winner of the Robert Louis Stevenson memorial award) would have been taken up by

London-based international publishing conglomerates (and thus gained the sales-creating clout of their marketing departments) without the example of books like *Morvern Callar*. Equally, the Edinburgh-based publishing houses Canongate and Polygon have begun to make stronger inroads into the UK market, with the "crossover potential" suddenly evident for Highlands-based writers like Michel Faber and Leila Aboulela. While it has to be emphasized that the spectacular sales success of *Trainspotting* is probably the single most influential factor here, it was the success of novels such as *Morvern Callar* which helped to convince publishers that *Trainspotting* was not simply an extraordinary exception to the rule.

5

Further Reading and Discussion Questions

DISCUSSION QUESTIONS

1. Do you think you need to feel an affinity with Morvern's lifestyle (her attitude to drink, drugs, casual sex) to enjoy the book? Do you generally prefer reading about characters who are like or unlike you? Warner's novels are generally focused around the lives of young, working-class women — do you think they are therefore inaccessible to older, middle-class readers?

2. Morvern has been described by many critics as "amoral" — do you think she is? Why do you think she conceals her boyfriend's suicide?

3. As narrator, Morvern goes to some lengths to conceal or deny her emotions from the reader — does this make it hard for you to identify with her as the book's central character? Do the gaps in the narrative disturb or intrigue you? Alan Warner has said that he was inspired by the narrative voice in Camus's novel *The Outsider* — can you compare the two narrative techniques?

4. How different do you think the book would be if it was narrated in the third person, so that you knew what other characters were thinking? Or if it started before Morvern's boyfriend's suicide, so that you "met" him as a character?

5. Morvern is a female narrator created by a male author — do you find her voice convincingly "female"? Can you compare it to other examples of male writers narrating in the voice of female characters, such as Roddy Doyle's *The Woman Who Walked Into Doors*, Martin Amis's *Night Train*, or Bernard MacLaverty's *Grace Notes*? What about when women write as men as, for instance, Annie Proulx tends to do, or as Carol Shields did in the Booker Prize-winning *Larry's Party*? Does the author's sex matter to you at all?

6. Unlike the majority of novels published in Britain, *Morvern Callar* is not written in "standard English." How important do you think this is for the book's overall effect on the reader? When you read books, do you normally "hear" the characters' voices in your head? If you've never been to Scotland, do you think the book's language creates a barrier to your enjoyment?

7. What effect do the book's extra-narrative devices — for example, Red Hanna's map, the inclusion of road signs, and the compilation tape track listings — have on your reading experience?

8. If you had been in charge of casting for the film of *Morvern Callar*, who would you have picked to play the main parts? Do you think film or television adaptations of novels normally work well?

BIBLIOGRAPHY

Novels by Alan Warner:

Morvern Callar (1995), which was shortlisted for the IMPAC Award and
     won a Somerset Maugham Award.
These Demented Lands (1997) which won an Encore Award.
The Sopranos (1998), which won The Saltire Award.
The Man Who Walks (2002).

Short Stories by Alan Warner:

"Yonder Cunt," "Blood of Eden," "A Spot of Night Fishing," "Smears 1,"
     "Smears 2," and "A Good Impression." All from *Folk: More Zoomers by
     Jim Ferguson, Alison Kermack, Gordon Legge, Alan Warner and Irvine
     Welsh*. Orkney: Clocktower Press, 1993.
"Costa Pool Bums." Available online at *www.barcelonareview.com/arc/r2/
     eng/costabum.htm.*
"After the Vision." In Kevin Williamson, *Children of Albion Rovers*. Edin-
     burgh: Rebel Inc., 1996.
"Bitter Salvage." In Sarah Champion, *Disco Biscuits*. London: Sceptre,
     1997
"Car Hung, Upside Down." In Duncan McLean, *Ahead of Its Time*. Lon-
     don: Vintage, 1998.
"At a Fair Old Rate of Knots." In *Edinburgh Review Issue 100*, ed. Sophy
     Dale. Edinburgh: Edinburgh University Press, 1999.
"Night Salient." Available online at *www.northwords.co.uk/sept2000.htm.*

Background Reading

Not all of these books deal with Warner directly, but those which
don't are useful background reading if you want to find out more
about contemporary Scottish writing.

Craig, Cairns. *The Modern Scottish Novel: Narrative and the National Imagination.* Edinburgh: Edinburgh University Press, 1997.

Crawford, Robert. *Devolving English Literature*, 2nd ed. Edinburgh: Edinburgh University Press, 2000.

Kravitz, Peter, ed. *The Picador Book of Contemporary Scottish Fiction.* London: Picador, 1997.

Leonard, Tom. *Intimate Voices: Selected Work 1965–1983.* Newcastle: Galloping Dog Press, 1984.

Leonard, Tom. *Reports From the Present: Selected Work 1982–94.* London: Jonathan Cape, 1995.

March, Christie Leigh. "Interview with A.L. Kennedy" and "Interview with Janice Galloway." In *Edinburgh Review Issue 101*, ed. Sophy Dale. Edinburgh: Edinburgh University Press, 1999.

McLean, Duncan. "Time Bombs: A Short History of the Clocktower Press." In McLean, *Ahead of Its Time.* London: Vintage, 1998.

Redhead, Steve. *Repetitive Beat Generation.* Edinburgh: Rebel Inc., 2000.

Sinfield, Alan. *Literature, Politics and Culture in Postwar Britain.* London: Athlone Press, 1997.

Wallace, Gavin and Randall Stevenson, eds. *The Scottish Novel Since the Seventies.* Edinburgh: Edinburgh University Press, 1993.

Websites

www.randomhouse.com/boldtype/0497/warner/interview.html — Bold Type interview.

www.spikemagazine.com/0300alanwarner.htm — an interview between Alan Warner and Zoë Strachan.

www.spikemagazine.com/0599queerspotting.htm — Zoë Strachan's essay on homosexuality in the work of Welsh and Warner.

www.richmondreview.co.uk/books/soprano.html — Polly Rance reviews *The Sopranos.*

www.barcelonareview.com/arc/r2/eng/warnerint.htm — *Barcelona Review* — interview.

www.barcelonareview.com/arc/r2/Bookcovers/covers2.htm — an essay/inter-

view on the British, American, and Spanish book cover designs for
Warner's first three novels.

www.barcelonareview.com/arc/r2/eng/artic5.htm—very useful essay by
Gustavo San Roman: "Alan Warner: The Scottish Onetti"

www.complete-review.com/reviews/warnera/morvern.htm—useful compen-
dium of reviews of *Morvern Callar* and links to other sites featuring
Alan Warner.

www.spoonrecords.com/alanwarner.html—a page on Warner as part of the
Can site.

Notes

1. This comment by Alan Warner, in common with all those which
follow in the text, with the obvious exception of quotations from the novels,
is taken from a series of interviews conducted both in person and by e-mail
between myself and Warner.

2. This comment, and the subsequent quotation from Robin Robertson,
are both taken from an interview conducted by e-mail in November 2001.